May 2023

Dear Elizabeth,

these are
your heart!
With friendship,
Christine Strittmatter

(Psalm 138:2)

The *Real Life* MOM:

52 Devotions to Cultivate Fruitful Living

By Christine Strittmatter

Pageant Wagon Publishing
Vineland, New Jersey

The Real Life Mom: 52 Devotions to Cultivate Fruitful Living
By Christine Strittmatter

ISBN: 978-1-7360080-2-7

Published by Pageant Wagon Publishing
Kathryn Ross, Publisher and Editor

ENDORSEMENTS

"Christine Strittmatter has written an inspiring work that will help you to navigate the daily challenges of life that try to rob us of our peace but cannot, if we do not allow them to do so. With compassion and insight, she points us to the One Who is always with us in the midst of every storm — the Lord Jesus Christ, the Lover of our Souls and the Savior of our Hearts. You will be blessed as you read this devotional. Keep it close by for continual encouragement as you go through your own life journey."

Dr. MaryAnn Diorio
Author of *The Italian Chronicles Trilogy*

"Christine Strittmatter has an authentic walk and relationship with Jesus Christ. Her genuine experiences as a Christian mom are evident in each devotional and will inspire you to walk faithfully with Christ. You will enjoy learning, through real-life experiences, what it means to live a fruitful, Christ-centered life."

Dr. Dawn Cobb-Fossnes
Applied Research Mentor and Adjunct Instructor
Liberty University

"Christine is a prolific and inspirational writer. As a previous student, she continues to impress me. Her devotionals can help lift and soothe your soul."

Dr. Ralph Fox II
Licensed Clinical Mental Health Counselor
Supervisor, IM/Assistant Professor at Liberty University

"*The Real Life Mom: 52 Devotions to Cultivate Fruitful Living* is an excellent devotional! Get ready to transform the next year of your life. Cultivate a year of growth by starting each week with one of the 52 wonderful stories that will take root in your heart. This book takes a genuine authentic approach of sharing everyday life experiences with a biblical worldview. They will encourage you to consider ways to live a Spirit-filled life. I would strongly recommend this book to anyone who has a desire to grow deeper in their faith."

Pastor Ken Corson
Fairton Christian Center

DEDICATION

Pamela Schiano—Couldn't have had a better sister. Your creative flair and confident outlook toward life were just what your *baby sister* needed. I love you with all my heart.

Robert Rice—I looked up to you, the older brother and protector. I missed you when you left for college and cherished your first letter to me on Brockport State University stationery—reading it over dozens of times. Forever thankful for you and love you with all my heart.

My husband, Dave—My first-rate encourager, listener, best friend, and more. How perfect—God's plan to plant us in the right place at the right time. No chance-meeting. I'm grateful for the godly man you are and looking forward to finishing our earthly race together. With my respect, thanks, & love—Always yours.

ACKNOWLEDGEMENTS

Paula Sheets—My beloved friend and confidante. Can't thank you enough for the numerous times you've encouraged me—in episodes of life and with my writing. God planted you in my life, a treasured friend and sister-in-Christ, who often read my heart like written words on a page. Thank you for your loving and faithful friendship through many decades.

Tina Volpe—Thank you for your encouragement as you've shared your appreciation for my writing. Just when I needed support, God used you to speak into my life. With friendship, love, and thanks.

Pastor Ken Corson—Thank you for following God's call upon your life and for your dedication to Him and Fairton Christian Center & Academy. Your life reflects your love for God and His people. With respect and appreciation for living what you teach and preach.

The late Pastor Woodson Moore—My former pastor who taught and lived the Word. He showed us, his congregants, the importance of cultivating a warrior-heart to navigate our Christian journey. Forever grateful.

Alison, Samuel, and Madeline—Shouting out a special thank you for your faithful support. What gifts! Knowing you've been in my corner to pray for me and believe in me means the world!

Kathryn Ross, my Editor and Publisher—Thank you for your confident voice offering support, guidance, and the specific touches to complete this project. May the Lord continue to bless your book shepherding services!

TABLE OF CONTENTS

A person's words can be life-giving water;
words of true wisdom are as refreshing
as a bubbling brook.
Proverbs 18:4 NLT

As an ordinary woman,
I carry an extraordinary message to you
as I live my real life
from a biblically-formed worldview.
My desire and motive
are to encourage and exhort you
while bringing hope to every situation
you may face in your life's journey.
Stay with me in your reading journey
as you cultivate growth
to produce fruitful living!

Christine Strittmatter

Introduction:
Cultivating God's Fruitful Living Gifts

For the wages of sin is death,
but the free gift of God is eternal life in Christ Jesus our Lord
Romans 6:23 ESV

Gifts!

We buy them. We wrap them. We give them. The anticipation builds. Will this gift be a winner? Will he like it? Will she keep it always?

Throughout my childhood, I received many gifts for varied occasions. Some of them I treasured, while others were less special. And then there were those gifts that I didn't even realize were gifts until much later in life.

For instance, the first gift I ever received—that any of us ever received—was the gift of life. God placed me, a tiny soul seed, in an imperfect family that was perfect for me. A fractured family where my parents lived separated into two houses for various reasons.

Mom attentively cared for my older sister, brother, and me. We enjoyed home-cooked meals and warm embraces after a long school day. In my adolescent years, I enjoyed a stylish wardrobe, a sacrificial expense paid off over time by my mother.

She was my anchor and provided stability in our modest living quarters, even though she faced adverse circumstances of her own. She generously poured into me, like a gardener watering a tender sprout, the gifts of unconditional love and selfless giving.

My father was a World War II Army veteran touched by the ravages of war. The trauma and loss he witnessed and experienced were invisibly stuffed inside the duffle bag he carried home with him. Even though it was difficult for him to say it aloud, I understood he loved me. I knew it in my soul from his actions—like how he patiently towel-dried my hair after baths and played catch with me in the backyard. My father introduced me to the relationship between a softball and leather glove which I sensed brought him joy as much as it watered me with his attention. I appreciated his calm demeanor when he taught me to drive a car with a standard transmission. The impact of his actions assured me of his love.

But those early years were missing the intimate knowledge of Christ because my parents couldn't give what or who they did not possess. I walked with my much-loved older siblings to Sunday school at a mainline denominational church. We sang hymns and read some Scripture—mostly Psalms. As a teen, when they no longer lived at home, I attended church by myself.

Even so, I didn't know God was reachable and touchable by faith, which handicapped me in the knowledge of Him as a narrative story only. I didn't Real Life know Him. I never learned about His Gift of new life in Christ from my parents at home, my school, or my experiences in church. I never understood what Psalm 139 taught about how God knows me and loves me through to the depth of my being. Take a moment and read Psalm 139 and consider—are you convinced of His deep love for you?

But somewhere, deep in my soul, the gift of God in my Real Life, the love I felt and received from my parents as they knew to give it enabled me to realize God's passion for me. Without my knowing it, God had planted a seed in my heart through the perfect yet imperfect influences of my family and early church experiences. This gift contained the rudiments necessary to bring forth fruit-bearing plants in my life—a seed planted in a pot that needed to be cultivated.

In my youthful season of life, God provided that cultivation through many teachers who watered the seed in my heart. In elementary school, a teacher warmly gathered our class to join her in song at the piano. Another teacher taught our class how to form alphabet letters with precision. I worked diligently to form my letters just right, and though some stood straight and tall while others curved in their own unique arcs, I still love to neatly print letters and write words as if on an artistic canvas.

Planted seeds. Cultivated. Growth.

In high school, a social studies teacher was able to reach me with enlivened lessons about people groups in Europe and Africa. He oversaw sensitive discussions of life and conditions in obscure lands as he paced animatedly in leather penny loafers and pointed to notes and diagrams on the chalkboard. His stories of faraway lands and people captivated my imagination.

A high school English teacher introduced me to classic literature. A favorite selection, *Les Miserables*, intrigued me with its message of redemption and sacrificial love. My teacher expanded my understanding of the world with the classics in contrast to my existent affection for Nancy Drew mysteries. Overall, my teachers left their mark on me because they believed in me when I'm sure I didn't believe in myself.

Planted seeds. Cultivated. Inspiration.

As I navigated the challenges of childhood and adolescence in upstate New York, I grappled with feelings of insecurity and inferiority. God planted me in a specific family structure, with the influence of schoolteachers and Saint Mark's Church to cultivate the seed in my heart.

But I had not learned I could lean on a Heavenly Father who would comfort and meet me in times of confusion, fear, and inadequacy. The soil of my life lacked the fertile nature necessary to continued growth. My root system hit sinking sand. If nothing changed in the cultivation of my life's soil, my growth would be stunted and eventually result in defeat—and death.

Even as a child, surrounded with the nurturing elements of home, school, and church, I matured to wonder, *Why do I feel so barren? Is this all life has to offer?* Please know this: God is merciful to us in our seedling being. He doesn't leave us barren if we cry out to Him with such questions.

In a gracious and loving manner God made Himself known to me. At the age of 21, I first learned about the Savior who wanted to be a Personal Resident in my heart and life. Profound love. A Divine Gardener whose very presence cultivates me with the daily gifts of His light and rains of refreshment towards fruitful living every day.

The soil of my heart in Him was barren no more, but fertile—something to cultivate in my relationship with God. I have since sought to tend the gift of my life from His hand into my adulthood and eventual motherhood. I planted the real of God into the Real Life of a mom. And now, I cultivate

5

the same in the lives of others who seek the fruitfulness of the Real Life Mom Lifestyle.

As a young one, were you gifted with the advantage of a Christ-centered home? If you were, you are beyond blessed. But, perhaps, like me, you were not. Guess what— you are still beyond blessed!

While our real lives in the earth may not be seeded with perfection, when Jesus takes up residence in your Real Life, your Real Life is cultivated in Him to produce abundant fruit. A fruitful tree or field ready to harvest or flower garden alive with vibrancy and color, each begins with a seed, set in soil and nurtured through water, light, and precise pruning. This is Real Life.

I believe the most important element of parenthood is to pass on the gift of our faith in Jesus Christ to our children, families, and all those God brings across our path in our Real Life. He is the only One who can meet their every need.

In *The Real Life Mom: 52 Devotions to Cultivate Fruitful Living,* I explore our lives as a bountiful garden that must be tended and cultivated in union with the Word and Will of God—first within our own seed hearts and then within our children's seed hearts and extended relationships. In this book, we'll explore the necessity of Soil, Water, Light, and Pruning to the purpose and produce a bountiful harvest.

Walk with me through this inspirational garden of 52 devotions as I share episodes from my years cultivating the fruit of the Spirit in my Real Life and seeding it into the lives of others. Take your time and read one a week or use the Table of Contents to read topically as you have need. Make use of the Consider questions to journal how you might apply what you learn to your Real Life and explore the

Scriptures in the Further Study sections. Add your own prayer to the one I've included. Also don't forget to check out the References listed at the end of the book. They may inspire you to look into some of the excellent resources that have informed me through the years in my ministry and writing.

Eventually you'll have cultivated fruitful living gifts of your own to give away. And isn't giving the gift often more rewarding than receiving it?

Warmly yours,
Christine Strittmatter
Summer 2022

8

SOIL

Seed Life in Christ,
planted
in a place of preparation
where roots plunge deep in Him
and are nourished.

Cultivating the Presence of God

You make known to me the path of life; in your presence there is fullness of joy; at your right hand are pleasures forevermore.
Psalm 16:11 ESV

At the time of this writing, my hand is swollen due to a freakish incident, and I'm experiencing nasty cold symptoms.

It began as an ordinary Thursday. I arrived at the school where I worked and as I closed the heavy car door, I walloped my outer hand against it, hard. Real hard. Immediately, it pulsated in pain, and I nearly saw stars.

I entered the building and walked down the hall to meet with my fellow teachers and my pastor as he was preparing to bring the morning devotion. After a few minutes, I noticed my hand had ballooned out of proportion. I didn't hear a word of the devotion after that, but waited to pronounce my predicament, "Excuse me, Pastor, will you please pray for my hand?"

After we left the meeting room, the staff peppered me with questions and concerns: "How can I help you?" "Do you need to see a doctor?" "Do you want to go home?"

"No, no, I'm staying."

A co-worker quickly brought ice to help with the swelling, another brought hot tea. The rollicking 9-11-year-old children in the classroom remained vigilant throughout the day and avoided any unintentional contact with my weird-looking hand. They took some pity on me when they noticed me nursing a few sniffles at the onset of a cold.

I survived the school day. *Thank You, Lord.*

Being a Thursday, I left school and headed to the local hospital. Not for medical attention, but because that was the day I volunteered in the pastoral care department. The chart was prepared and waiting for me with nearly 30 patients to visit.

At one of the nurses' stations, I stopped to inquire about my hand. She looked at it and promptly confirmed, "It's a hematoma. You'll be okay."

Thank You, Lord.

I completed the visitation rounds, drove home and reflected on my day. The reliable and constant presence of God was recognizable from beginning to end:

- A faithful and faith-filled pastor and staff were present to pray for me minutes after the mishap.
- A parent dropping off her child at school in the morning saw my hand as she was leaving the building and casually remarked that it looked like a hematoma. Her nonchalance was somewhat supportive for me as I had never seen this kind of swelling before.
- A co-worker swiftly presented me with ice and a wrap to apply to the bruised area.
- Another staff member brought me hot tea.
- The children were conscientious as they and I moved about the classroom that day.
- The skillful nurse allayed my fears about my swollen hand that all would be well.

Just another day in the Kingdom of God where He showed himself present in His goodness to me. No matter what kind of day I may have, or freakish accident befall me, I can say with all my heart, mind, soul, and strength that God is good. He is good and brings me through every trial. He finds me—and will find you—every minute of the day no matter if the day involves a swollen hand, nasty cold symptoms after a long day at work, and volunteer duty.

Consider:
We all encounter trials in our lives—many times unexpected ones that may include deep waters or fires of oppression. What life moments proved to you God's presence to carry you through? Reflect on these and journal them as a permanent record to bolster your courage to face your tomorrows.

Further Reading:
Trials of life, deep waters, fires of oppression—Isaiah 43:2

Prayer:
Father, though I may not feel in my body the joy of Your presence, I know You're with me to see me through even trying situations as You've proven Yourself countless times. Thank You for Your steadfast faithfulness and honorability. Amen.

Cultivating Loving Ties that Bind

*And now I am going to Jerusalem, drawn there irresistibly by the
Holy Spirit, not knowing what awaits me there, except that the
Holy Spirit has told me in city after city that jail and suffering lie
ahead. But my life is worth nothing unless I use it for doing the
work assigned me by the Lord Jesus — the work of telling others
the Good News about God's wonderful kindness and love.*
Acts 20:22-24 NLT

How do we cultivate a loving tie with the Holy Spirit
that binds us snugly to Him?

Decades ago, I agreed to bind with Jesus and walk in
a close-fitting personal journey. I learned I had to release
religion and in exchange, embrace a Person.

This was similar to my experience upon enlistment in
the military. Although submitting to military standards
cannot compare to following the Holy Spirit's lead, the
analogy fits.

When I took the Armed Services Oath, I stepped over
the line from civilian life into a military environment. There
was actually a tangible line the officer asked me to step
across once I agreed to this decision. Paraphrasing the
gentleman, once I stepped over the line he announced, "You
now belong to the United States military/Navy — to defend

the Constitution bound by the Uniform Code of Military Justice." Although his words jolted me, I willingly agreed.

As I transitioned from Basic Training to technical schools to future duty stations, I put my trust in the military. They moved me from place to place where the mission needed me. I could fill out a "dream sheet," a request for a desired location if the military agreed, but I never knew where I'd be sent or what awaited me there.

I experienced distressful episodes as I learned to adapt to military culture. Being a woman minority in a field dominated by men was challenging, but I wouldn't quit or lose heart. My soul may have quaked, but I would not desert my commitment or the charge before me.

Embracing discipline, teamwork, and unified spirit toward one purpose, I completed my enlistment time strong. Far from home and family, I had bound myself to a military life to fulfill a significant mission.

In Acts 20, Scripture explains how Paul was constrained by the Holy Spirit to fulfill a harrowing mission prepared by God. He was led step by step, from one city to the next, from one audience to another, to bind himself close to the divine lead.

Several important themes from Acts 20 point to the benefits of Paul's being bound in the spirit as he headed for Jerusalem. We can learn much from Paul's behavior as he cultivated a binding and lasting tie to the Holy Spirit:

1. Paul secured a personal relationship with the Holy Spirit to ensure safety as he followed His lead. This binding relationship developed over time and connected them so close that he could recognize the

Spirit's promptings. This is necessary for believers who desire intimacy with their Savior.

2. Paul learned to trust the Holy Spirit even when he didn't know what would happen in the future. He mastered moving forward following the prod of the Spirit.

3. Paul received comfort when the Spirit forewarned that he would face afflictions. Even as such days were prepared before him, he didn't need to fear. With a tumultuous future pending, he resolved not to faint.

4. Paul finished life strong and achieved his goal to valiantly fulfill his God-designed purpose.

Being bound to the Lord releases us from our own insecurities. We'll not encounter the trials Paul did, but we do experience hardships.

Let's resolve to bind with God to faithfully complete our personal journeys. We can have glorious lives in Christ!

Consider:
Describe how you are bound to God's Spirit unified with Him. What ways will you cultivate more intimate ties with Holy Spirit who will never misdirect you?

Further Reading:
Paul's intimate relationship with the Holy Spirit—Acts 20

Prayer:
Father, as I bind together with You, I am safely embraced in Your loving grip. May I continue to know Your voice and respect Your leadership as I share and spread Your name. Amen.

Cultivating Prayer Time

My heart has heard you say, "Come and talk with me."
And my heart responds, "LORD, I am coming."
Psalm 27:8 NLT

Morning is my favorite time to meet with God. I appreciate the days I don't have to scurry off to work, so I can linger longer, lounging in my pajamas, enjoying quiet time. Although it may take a while for me to come to life after I've woken from the night's sleep, eventually I settle into my quiet place.

In my upstairs' bedroom, I prop myself up with a couple of comfy pillows, a light blanky, my cup of favorite hot tea, and my Bible, notebook, and pencil. If it's still darkish, I open the curtains to scan the sunrise and listen to the chattering birds. Alone, I feel the quiet of the room and am often aware of a slight smile on my face. I've created a warm, cozy, safe place, uninterrupted by the world. A sanctuary.

What a difference a few minutes set aside in prayer makes! As I sit undistracted before the Lord, I allow my heart to be quieted and gaze upon Jesus. If my hands are chilled in crisp weather seasons, they're warmed as He stills my mind and spirit.

Focused reflection upon God's goodness illuminates His grace in my life and I know peace in the place of prayer. I expect God will show up when I meet Him in my "secret place" and anticipate how He will:

- help me
- direct me
- ground me if circumstances buffet me on unstable terrain
- teach me what I don't understand
- be merciful to me
- heal me
- fulfill His promises to me

Psalm 37:23 ESV states, "The steps of a man are established by the LORD, when he delights in his way." After a few minutes of communion with the Lord in prayer, my heart is filled with gratitude to see how God orders my steps.

Here are some of the benefits I've discovered when I take a mere fifteen minutes in prayer:

- Quiets my heart and mind
- Brings awareness of God's presence
- Alerts me to God's concerns rather than what's been rattling my thoughts
- Puts life in perspective
- Presents opportunity to pray for others
- Refreshes and energizes my soul and spirit
- Fosters an intimate love for my Heavenly Father
- Creates a passion to honor and obey Him

This intimate prayer time is for my benefit. I feel His pleasure. It isn't always 15 minutes long, but it is a daily, intentional engagement with my Father God. No one tells me to do it. I want to invest this established time to draw close to Him and nourish my spirit. As James 4:8 affirms, when I draw close to the Lord, He draws nearer to me, too. It's the favorite part of my day.

Consider:

Describe your "secret place" prayer-closet. How have your prayer encounters with God changed you? How have you experienced the glow of God's peace and order in your steps as you make time to unite with Him in prayer? If you don't have 15 minutes, bask in the few moments you do have and consider the impact of His presence as you commune together.

Further Reading:

David's sanctuary—Psalm 26:6-8

Prayer:

Father, thank You for the gift of prayer—a time of personal connection with You. It reveals to me Your path and direction for my life and allows me to privately meet with You. Amen.

Cultivating Confidence in Prayer Like Jesus

So they took away the stone. And Jesus lifted up His eyes and said, "Father, I thank You that You have heard Me. I knew that You always hear Me, but I said this on account of the people standing around, that they may believe that You sent Me."
John 11:41-42 ESV

Relationally, we grow as close to Jesus as we want. We determine this.

As we ingest the Word via daily meetings with God, we learn to know His voice, we discover His desires for us, and recognize His promptings to do or not to do this thing or that. Our confidence soars resulting in being able to trust God hears us. He always hears us.

While dating for a year before our marriage, my soon-to-be husband in New Jersey called me practically every evening. Residing in New York, some 325 miles away, I expected and anticipated the call from him. Because he called so frequently, I knew his voice without the need for him to identify himself.

Similar to recognizing my husband's voice, I perceive God's voice and nudging as I routinely read the Scriptures. My heart is turned in His direction. As I seek Him in patience, I trust to hear from Him. And I do.

To cultivate our confidence in personal prayer encounters, we must commit to continually grow in relationship with the Lord. We entreat Him using His authority, we decree Scriptural promises, and we restrain the enemy through the power of God's written Word, spoken aloud.

Praying with God's Authority

As our relationship with God grows and fortifies, we learn and practice praying with authority in Jesus' Name as granted to us, notably recorded in Luke 9:49-50 and Acts 3:6,16. It is as if He awarded us His power of attorney to legally and lawfully execute orders. When believers in Christ appeal to God, they confidently pray in agreement with biblical Scriptures. In this way, believers depend on God to keep His Word, as He cannot lie.

Proclaiming and Decreeing

We're convinced God hears us when we proclaim and decree His Word. For instance, if we feel threatened or fearful of a person or situation, we proclaim aloud a Scripture such as Proverbs 29:25 ESV stating, "The fear of man lays a snare, but whoever trusts in the Lord is safe." We personalize that verse and ordain it over ourselves announcing, "The fear of others is a trap, but I live safely when I believe and receive God's safety." As we meditate on it and other Scriptures pertaining to fear, our faith enlarges.

We can pray for protection during wartime for military servicemen/women, declaring Psalm 91:7 ESV, "A thousand may fall at your side, ten thousand at your right hand, but it will not come near you." Personalizing that verse and speaking it aloud as legislation sounds like,

"Hordes may fall all around me, but I won't be sabotaged by evil."

Restraining the Enemy

As Christ-followers, we have authority to restrain the enemy of our souls, Satan. He strives to steal and destroy the gratifying things God intends for us. Satan is a master liar and attempts to squash the truth of Scriptural promises via his lies—the propaganda of hell. We combat him using the Word of God and speak it with the authority God imparted to us through salvation in Jesus Christ. Jesus illustrated this when declaring Scriptures to Satan's face when He was tempted, as recorded in Luke 4:1-14. God didn't leave us alone on earth without the instruction and tools to fight and resist the enemy of our souls. Remember, we do not fight against flesh and blood. Our enemy is Satan and his demonic forces.

To recap, cultivating confidence in prayer includes committing to deepen our relationship with the Lord, utilizing God's authority in prayer, decreeing Scriptural promises, and prohibiting Satan's attempted blockades in God's purposes in our life, the lives of our loved ones, and in all the earth.

Consider:

How will your prayers to your Heavenly Father become more confident and expectant? If you haven't been praying with the authority granted from the Father, how will you begin to do so? Don't be shy; God longs to hear from us and is pleased when we place our faith in Him.

Further Reading:

God cannot lie—Numbers 23:19; Titus 1:2

Our fight is against unseen evil spirits—Ephesians 6:12
Jesus' example when addressing Satan—Luke 4:1-14

Prayer:
Father, thank You for unfailingly knowing and hearing us—for the assurance we have as our prayers are reached and heard by You. We entreat You with eagerness and expectation. Amen.

Cultivating Surrender to God's Will

. . . I carry out the will of the one who sent me, not my own will.
John 5:30b NLT

Jesus Christ was born to die. As He sought His Father's perfect will in the Garden of Gethsemane, He endured a great foreboding.

Jesus was born both as the Son of God and as a man to identify with humanity. He sought to please God by doing His will. From the time He was a young man of 12 years old, He taught religious teachers in the Temple in Jerusalem declaring the Truth God had placed in His heart. As Luke 2:49 records, after Jesus and his parents had become separated in Jerusalem, He explained to his mother that He had to tend to His Father's business—an indication of His single-minded obedience to His Father God in Heaven.

Jesus also withstood staggering temptations from the devil because of His heart's surrender to God. Being provoked for forty days in the desert without any food, Jesus resisted the devil's temptations for earthly power and prominence using Scripture to quench him. The Bible states the devil withdrew. But he would eventually return.

As Jesus grew to adulthood, He boldly healed people on Sabbath days, which resulted in conflict with religious leaders regarding their oppressive, legalistic protocols.

Doing the will of God, He forgave men and women of grave sins and proclaimed that He was the Son of Man, which infuriated the teachers of religious law. As He ministered on the earth, Jesus chose to comply with God's purposes and endured the ridicule, rejection, and rebuke from religious figureheads.

In Gethsemane, Jesus wrestled with the choice God laid before Him, faced with a decision no human has ever had to confront. He surrendered to the will of God to fulfill His earthly mandate to lay down His life for all humanity as the propitiation for man's sin. A grueling death in the form of physical pulverization and ultimate crucifixion, after false accusation and public humiliation before mocking crowds, awaited Him.

According to Matthew 26:38-39, in the garden, we hear His humanity speak as He confesses to His disciples that His ". . . soul is exceedingly sorrowful, even to death" and to His Father in Heaven, ". . . if it is possible, let this cup pass from Me; nevertheless, not as I will, but as You will."
He pushed through this critical moment to make a world transforming choice—the full surrender unto death of His life in obedience to the will of God the Father. In doing so, he endured the heartache of one disciple betraying Him to the authorities, another publicly disowning Him, and the rest of the disciples abandoning Him to the mob, chief priests, and elders who wished to kill Him.

Even as Jesus invoked His Father a second time, petitioning if the cup of suffering be unavoidable, He was willing to follow through so the Father's will would be accomplished. Left alone, Jesus sustained betrayal, arrest, persecution, and injustice.

While it is true humanity crucified Jesus, He willingly surrendered His life because of His love for all. His shed blood trickled liquid love. Scripture states He could have called on "twelve legions of angels" to rescue Him but chose not to do so. As paraphrased in Matthew 26:52-54, by His own will He laid down His life as payment for our sin and fulfilled God's awesome plan of redemption and *life* restored.

The gruesome crucifixion precipitated the glorious resurrection! The resurrection completed Jesus' purpose while walking in the earth, empowering mankind the choice for a restored relationship with God. Reconciliation between God and humanity now is realized. Ultimate grace unwrapped in the Person of Jesus Christ.

How about us? How can we learn from the example of Jesus, totally surrendered to the will and purposes of God? How does that translate into the choices we make in the circumstances of real life on earth every day?

Choose to boldly foster life into your situations and family relationships by surrender to God's will and ways as guided in His Word. Just as God's grace empowered Jesus in His humanity to prevail in spiritual surrender, God provides the grace necessary to prevail in the everyday challenges we face. He fully equips us to make godly, willful choices to be more than overcomers and take hold of His reward when we choose life—living God's way.

When we are faced with tough circumstances and decisions, be strong and courageous to do what Scripture instructs and follow the example of Jesus—submitting our will to the will of the Father.

Consider:
Jesus is the primary example of surrender to the will of God and the ultimate fruitfulness of that choice. Consider these other biblical examples of the surrender to God's will and purposes and journal your thoughts:

Godly Willful Biblical Examples:
- Joseph resisted Potiphar's wife's lustful seduction (Genesis 39)
- Rahab sheltered two spies sent out by Joshua (Joshua 2)
- Jael courageously slew Sisera (Judges 4)
- David refused to kill King Saul when he had reason and opportunity (1 Samuel 24)
- Esther audaciously spoke truth to King Ahasuerus on behalf of her nation (Esther 5)
- The wayward son returned home; his father received and reinstated him (Luke 15)
- Jesus yielded Himself to the Father and ultimately to the cross (Matthew 27; Mark 15)

In contrast, the Bible also illustrates the negative outcomes of a human will not surrendered to godly choices:

Deadly Willful Biblical Examples:
- Adam and Eve sinned in the Garden of Eden (Genesis 3)
- Potiphar's wife desired Joseph (Genesis 39)
- Saul consulted a witch at Endor, an abomination to God (1 Samuel 28)
- David lusted after Bathsheba (2 Samuel 11)
- David sinned against Uriah resulting in Uriah's death (2 Samuel 11)

- Judas betrayed Jesus (Matthew 26)
- Religious and political leaders—humanity—crucified Jesus Christ (Matt. 27)
- An angry mob stoned Stephen to death (Acts 7)

Prayer:
Father, thank You for being our loving example as You selflessly chose to do Your Father's will. May we yield our strong wills into Your mighty hands as we determine our everyday choices. Amen.

Cultivating Our Identity in Christ

. . . work out your own salvation with fear and trembling, for it is
God who works in you, both to will and to work
for His good pleasure.
Philippians 2:12b-13 ESV

When does a person's life become valuable?

Our value is first established at conception—before we are newly born. We're fashioned in God's image as unique creations. Psalm 139 explains we're incredibly and elaborately woven within our mothers' wombs. God envisioned our reality and beheld us before anyone else could. Our lives are a miracle.

Similarly, to illustrate the concept of value on a small-scale, a craftswoman using her imagination initially visualizes and prepares to knit the unique creation she desires. She captures the design in her mind. This occurs before she takes the first stitch. She begins the masterpiece with each stitch until it is perfectly completed.

As a young woman, God saw me as a dear soul of great worth. But I lived out my identity molded from my own thoughts and intellect—and the estimation and opinions of others.

But when I accepted Christ as my Savior, I became born again and my identity changed. The Scripture in 2

Corinthians 5 describes this transformation as abandoning our old life serving ourselves in order to identify by faith with Christ in our new life. I became a new created being in Christ. The old nature was left behind and my life was made new in Him.

How did I begin to cultivate my identity with Christ?

The life and identity God intends for us is nestled in the Scriptures. As we read, study, and personalize the truths, the cultivation process forms. James 1 explains how we look into the Scriptures like we would gaze into a mirror—we see who we are, who we are bound to become. We embrace and act upon it. Otherwise, it is as if we look into a mirror, then walk away forgetting what we just saw.

Once I became a new creation in Christ, I discovered the cultivation of my identity in Him as a continual process of sanctification—becoming more Christ-centered. I continue to learn who God is and how He wants me to live life as I study the Bible.

I attended a church assembly with others who were hungry for God—eager to learn more about a personal God. I was discipled by spending time with seasoned Christians, those who already knew Him. Discipleship offers a new believer in Christ an opportunity to develop an intimate relationship with her newly found Savior. This occurs by delving deeper into biblical truths to gain better understanding and context of the Scriptures. I continue to yield myself to Jesus—to lean closer into Him.

How do I lean close to God, my personal Savior?

When I lean close to Jesus, it's similar to my trying to hear the announcements at a noisy airport terminal. I listen carefully when I have to connect flights. I incline myself to hear the airline employees as they announce the gate, the boarding time, and any flight changes. With undivided attention, I glean information to secure the connection. I cancel all other interference straining to hear the news, so I can ultimately act on it to reach my final destination.

What are some faith confessions I speak to cultivate my healthy identity in Christ?

My faith confessions must agree with the truth in the Word of God:

- I'm created in Your image, Lord. (Genesis 1:27)
- I'm marvelously and masterfully made by You. (Psalm 139:14)
- I'm the apple of Your eye. (Deuteronomy 32:10; Psalm 17:8)
- I eagerly await a hope and a future. (Jeremiah 29:11-14a)
- God, You love me with an everlasting love. (Jeremiah 31:3)
- I'm Your special Treasure, Lord. (Deuteronomy 14:2)
- You rescue me because You delight in me, Father. (Psalm 18:19)

What does false identity look like?

Our misaligned identities are the result of our limited and imperfect perception of ourselves in addition to lies from Satan. Some of these twisted identities are measured by our performance centered on our success, our titles, professional positions, and/or education. Others include our appearance, possessions, wealth, and/or places we frequent like restaurants and upscale clothing shops. Our reputation, popularity, and other people's opinions of us can be faulty measuring sticks, too.

Proverbs 18:11 describes how wealthy people can mistakenly think their riches represent safety. There's nothing wrong with professional position, possessions, or looking great, but don't fall into these traps and allow your identity to be falsified or stolen.

Jesus wants us to find our identity in Him. He cherishes us and considers us His special treasure and joy.

If you find yourself struggling with identity issues, be hopeful. Our journeys with Jesus are life-long adventures. Let Him live big in you, surrender to Him and grow in grace, as His presence touches the world through you!

Consider:

As you search the Scriptures, find more nourishing nuggets to confess as your identity in Christ continues to cultivate. After you locate these, write them down, meditate on them, and speak them aloud. Because they'll be built on truth, they will boost your faith and build your identity in Christ.

Further Reading:

Creation of man—Genesis 1:27 and 2:7

Misaligned perception of wealth—Proverbs 18:11

Our life and being in God—Acts 17:28

New life in Christ—2 Corinthians 5

God works in us for His pleasure and glory—Philippians 2:13

Be a doer, not just a hearer of the Bible—James 1

Prayer:

Father, may our Christian walk honor You as our identities continue to align with You. With reverential fear and trembling, we recognize that You're working in us to accomplish this. Thank You. Amen.

Cultivating Obedience:
Who or What Do We Follow?

For we live by believing and not by seeing.
2 Corinthians 5:7 NLT

Well trained dogs know the will of their masters well. They sense the desire of their masters as they walk beside them by the way the lead is managed. Dogs are trained not to give place to impulsive, emotional triggers that distract them from obeying the instructions of their master conveyed through the lead—a simple gesture or voice command. Dogs see where to go and know how to behave not with their natural eyes, but by faith in the direction and communication from their master, earning them favor and reward.

Unless, of course, you are Keira.

"Keira, come back!"

This was our plea when our son, in his white athletic socks, chased our little Cairn Terrier nearly a quarter mile across a freshly plowed farm when we first acquired her. She was cute, untrained, and not yet quite cuddly. Keira had a bad habit of darting out our back door when we opened it. Her sneaky escapes and unschooled ways required our loving investment of time and teaching to ensure harmonious living.

Not long after she came to live with us, she darted out the back door again at the sound of a mail truck. All 13 pounds of her charged down the driveway and slammed into the truck's wheel which bounced her back onto our driveway, injured with a bloody belly. A trip to the vet mended her flesh, but more work to secure her in spirit was ahead.

On her leash, Keira can walk in safety and in peace when she is obedient to follow my lead. But if she is tempted by a visual distraction—for instance, the guiltless mailman in his jeep—she barks, pulls in her own direction, and tries to escort me! This results in her gagging and choking as I halt her in her tracks. Gently, yet securely, I redirect her back on our walking path. I require her obedience, even as I feel her strong will get in the way on the taut lead.

When Keira stubbornly pulls away from my side because she feels she needs to sniff at a dirty hole, it reminds me how tethered we need to be with our living, loving Savior. Our yielded connectedness to God benefits us and glorifies Him. In God's phenomenal love, He has made it possible for you and me to live a favored life through faith, able to see beyond our natural eyes, too. If we impetuously become diverted by ideas or situations God has not intended for us, He gently, yet securely, redirects us, and we are wise to follow his shepherding lead. We thrive, as Keira can also, when we obediently walk by faith versus impulsively reacting when triggered by what we see with our eyes.

As a dog follows her master's lead, touch, and direction communicated, we can be led by God-ordained thoughts and the good fruit of our subsequent obedience to His will. In so doing, we are positioned in the Holy Spirit to

live in a peaceful, confident, joyful relationship with our
Lord.

Consider:

Keep a journal to log your forward, victorious steps to walk
by faith, believing, and not always by sight. This may serve
you as it has served me. The important thing is to follow
God's Truth, obedient in all things.

Further Reading:

The wise heed instruction—Proverbs 10:17
The righteous fall, yet always rise—Proverbs 24:16

Prayer:

*Father, may I be content knowing that I must walk by faith
believing and pliant to your lead, while imagining the humbling
day when I will see you Face to face. Amen.*

Cultivating a Warrior

The God of heaven will help us succeed. We his servants will start rebuilding this wall . . . Don't be afraid of the enemy! Remember the Lord, who is great and glorious, and fight for your friends, your families, and your homes!
Nehemiah 2:20; 4:14b NLT

Warriors don't complain about a hurdle, predicament, or injustice. They venture to contribute a working plan or a viable solution—at times sacrificially. Nehemiah proved to be one of these effective warriors.

Nehemiah, a Scriptural example of a trustworthy and influential warrior from the Old Testament, was an ordinary man called to oversee an extraordinary project. He contributed organizational leadership skills, plans, and an uncompromised stance to rebuild the broken walls around Jerusalem.

What did this warrior—or what would any warrior—need to do to cultivate the leader within?

Three distinguishing characteristics were evident in this noble warrior-leader's relationship with God:

- He prayed to a God he knew—intimately.
- He entreated God's help—humbly with confidence.
- He invited God into his decision-making as he accepted His counsel.

36

Nehemiah also understood the significance of a mind set to his tasks:

- To move forward with a project that appeared impossible
- To complete a task with opposition from enemies
- To remain undisturbed in spirit—choosing to exchange a prayer in place of a care
- To lead his team to finish the mission, as well as reorient the nation toward spiritual revival and religious makeover
- To award all the glory to God for the successful completion of the rebuilt wall

With a unified team of workers and God's blessing, Nehemiah led God's people to complete their assignment in record time.

My late pastor taught and trained the congregants and the students at our church and Christian school to be warriors in God's Kingdom. He emphasized similar warrior-attributes like Nehemiah's including:

- Pray timid-less prayers
- Yield to God's counsel
- Cultivate clean minds and hearts
- Seek God in decision-making

Let's be strong and courageous in the Lord—doing the work and tasks assigned us by God with His Spirit and truth abiding in us. We combat and obstruct the enemy's thievery, guarding what the Lord purchased for us by His once-and-for-all sacrifice on the cross. This is why we celebrate each year on Resurrection Sunday. We remember His ultimate, selfless gift for humanity and the empowerment He gives us to establish His Kingdom on earth as it is in Heaven.

As we cultivate our warrior within, similar to Nehemiah, we acknowledge God for our direction and assistance as we submit ourselves to Him. When enemies emerge and assail us with evil intentions, we stand in our endowed authority, equipped with our spiritual weapons.

We resist moving with revenge. God is our defense — and offense. As Romans 12:19 assures us, He promises to secure justice. Vengeance belongs to Him — He will compensate in due season.

Consider:

It's important to recognize our warrior characteristics and imperative for us to behave like warriors — being doers and workers in our spheres of influence. What warrior attributes do you currently possess? How might you plan to cultivate some of the warrior-leader qualities described in this devotional?

Further Reading:

Vengeance is God's undertaking — Romans 12:19

Prayer:

Father, I'm privileged to be Your warrior, and I thank You for residing within me so I don't face battles alone. May I be about Your business to do the work I'm called to do with integrity and with deference to You, resisting the enemy. Amen.

Cultivating Spiritual Weapons

For though we walk in the flesh, we are not waging war according to the flesh. For the weapons of our warfare are not of the flesh but have divine power to destroy strongholds.
2 Corinthians 10:3-4 ESV

While preparing for battle, military soldiers are always trained to respect their weapons—how to use them, how to disassemble and reassemble them, how to clean them, how to secure them, and ultimately how to pull the trigger for effect. They would never arrive on the battlefield without their weapons.

My natural tendency is to keep the peace. Don't make too many waves and walk in peace to the best of my ability. This is Scriptural. Even so, the Word of God says we have an enemy, we are in a life and death war situation, and there are times we must fight—resisting the enemy, equipped to pull the trigger. We wrestle for that which belongs to us.

As believers in Christ, we've inherited spiritual weapons. These weapons assist us to fight the good fight of faith. We're appointed to contend for the faith, and there will be times we must engage in spiritual battle.

Our most formidable spiritual weapon is the Name of Jesus, spoken by believers with the authority Jesus granted His people after His resurrection. Speak boldly in Jesus'

Name, the Name above all other names, as He instructed us to do and as the Book of Acts illustrates.

We implement the Name of Jesus as a power of attorney—it's not in our name, in our strong-will, in our ability or with our resources. We speak the Name of Jesus knowing the power in His Name results in answered prayers and breakthroughs. When aligning our prayer requests with biblical promises, we confidently rely on God to fulfill His promised Word. Using this spiritual weapon, the prayer may sound like: *Father, in the Name of Jesus, the Scripture states You give strength when weak or weary. So, I take the authority You've pledged to me and ask You to grant me strength to complete the tasks You've called me to accomplish. Thank You. I receive Your endurance, vigor, and resilience. Amen.*

Other Forms of Spiritual Weaponry

Praise: God inhabits—dwells in—our praises. It's most important for us to praise when we feel least inclined. As the late Bible teacher and author, Derek Prince, explained: "Our praises silence the enemy of our souls."

Personal and Corporate Prayer: Prayer expresses our heart's requests, thanksgiving, and laments. We're instructed to pray at all times, including prayer for one another.

Fasting: On numerous occasions, Jesus taught His followers to couple fasting with prayer as weapons of defense. The added element of fasting—abstaining from food for a certain amount of time—serves to filter us. It clarifies a warrior's mind and spirit.

Thankfulness/Gratefulness: Illustrated in Luke 17:11-19, Jesus emphasized the importance of thankfulness when He referred to one out of ten lepers who returned to offer thanks for his healing. Psalm 100:4 also affirms how we first give thanks as we enter a time of praise and worshipful singing to God.

Love: Love builds bridges. Jesus' great desire of divine rule in our hearts was for us to love Him and each other. He told his disciples that they would be recognized as His followers when they loved well. Love is a commanding decision and action–it breaks down barriers and chasms that divide people.

As our prime example, Jesus patterned the way for us as He implemented these spiritual weapons of praise, prayer, fasting, thankfulness, love, and more when He lived and showed The Way on the earth.

Therefore, stand up, wield your weapon, and address the enemy of your soul who comes to afflict and devastate. Take aim, pull the trigger, and submit to God, resisting the devil who then must flee. When you've done all you know to do, stand fast in peace and security remaining in a trust-position. There will be sweet victories after battles, but do not be surprised if the thief later returns with other schemes. Take heart and learn to battle wisely using the weapons of your warfare. As you use these weapons, you will become more proficient.

Consider:
Be mindful that we can have much Scriptural knowledge, but if we do not apply it to life situations during warfare-trials, it is ineffective against the enemy of our souls. What

weaponry will you proactively wield when the enemy assails you in the future?

Further Reading:
Contend for our faith—Matthew 11:12
Maintain peace with one another, as best as you can—Romans 12:18
Submit to God and resist the enemy—James 4:7
God provides strength—Psalm 18:31-33; Psalm 29:11
God is our strength—Psalm 18:1; Psalm 28:7
The Name of Jesus Christ—Acts 3:6, 3:16, 4:10, 4:18, 4:30
Love One Another—John 13:34-35, 15:12
Two Love Commandments—Matthew 22:36-40

Prayer:
Father, I appreciate that You have made provision for me to effectively fight spiritual battles. Our enemy is in the unseen realm, so we use the spiritual weapons You've designed for us to demolish corrupt and unholy barriers. Amen.

Cultivating Joy in Battle

Yes, the LORD has done amazing things for us! What joy!
Psalm 126:3 NLT

Although life holds trials and difficulties, we learn from Scripture that the Christian is in the world, but not of the world. Some will experience more trials, pain, and difficulties than others; nevertheless, all will endure some hardships. It sounds paradoxical, but we have the opportunity to live a blessed life with joy even with challenges and struggles of different kinds.

I have a friend who has withstood her share of hardships. She's a beautiful illustration of one who's endured trials and preserved a joyful heart. She is widowed and has sustained the loss of an adult child.

While homebound for more than two years because of physical challenges, she renewed her love and practice of painting. Her home is like an art gallery arrayed with paintings of family members, wildlife, friends, rustic scenery, and her Savior Jesus. Because she gifts many of these treasures to family and friends, others experience joy from her talent.

Even though she lives at home alone, she makes it a point not to isolate herself. She's surrounded by many loving family members, in addition to oodles of friends—

both young and old. My friend nourishes her mind and spirit as she daily studies her Bible and connects thoughtfully with people via social media. She's eager to pray with much empathy for hurting people. With her generous heart to consider others, she experiences joy no matter her many losses in life.

One main thing I notice about this woman is her wittiness. She's quick to lighten up a conversation as she cultivates joy in her battle. She exercises her laughter muscles and helps others to chuckle, too. Scripture teaches that a merry heart is like a medicine, so it's safe to say that laughter is a workout for her in soul and spirit!

At the same time, I remain aware and don't discount the possibility that even in her laughter her soul may ache. Proverbs 14:13 explains how laughter can camouflage a heavy heart. Nevertheless, this woman survives and thrives as a good soldier of Jesus Christ. Her aim, as illustrated in 2 Timothy 2, is to please the One who enlisted her.

Like my friend, we, too, are called to war for joy. Jesus is our prime example as we observe His decision-making to cultivate joy in His battle. During His ministry years, He forsook sleep and sometimes food as He communed with His Heavenly Father. He tended to multitudes of suffering people—broken in body, spirit, and mind. These were His desires and choices—He didn't complain or resist. His Father knew Him, and He knew His Father and the divine assignment.

In His service to others, Jesus also offered a better life to prostitutes, demon-possessed people, and outcasts—for both life on earth and for a future eternal existence. He endured grueling temptations from the evil one maintaining

His focus on the mission and love for His Father and humanity. There was joy in this battle.

Jesus celebrated with others when He took time to attend weddings, to enjoy children providing His undivided attention, and to feed people physically and spiritually. He traveled around preaching to crowds and counseling individuals, while imparting light, joy, and hope. Jesus attracted people to Himself like a magnet because He was anointed by God.

He exalted and honored His Father God in all these encounters.

As I cultivate joy, I experience great contentment in knowing God, knowing God loves me, and sharing Him with others. I'm centered as I safeguard close fellowship with Him and meditate on the exceptional things He's done. Appreciating the blessing of my family and friends, each one of them with their special uniqueness, brings much delight. Even as adversities and troubles of life assail, I war for joy as I serve God and others with the talents and giftings He's given me to fulfill my purpose.

Decide to war for joy regularly. Our Savior provided all we need to complete our earthly journey well as we honor God.

Consider:
What are some specific ways you personally contend for joy? Do you recall a past situation when you could have chosen joy rather than not, thus realizing God's goodness in a victory? If so, journal or share it with a trusted friend.

Further Reading:
A cheerful heart is good medicine — Proverbs 17:22a

In the world, but not of the world—John 17
Always be joyful—1 Thessalonians 5:16
All will endure hardships—1 Peter 4:19
Good soldier of Jesus Christ—2 Timothy 2
The Lord has done great things—Joel 2:21

Prayer:
Father, thank You for Jesus' faithful examples to cultivate joy in His many battles in this earthly realm. Jesus, You've done amazing things as You served others while on earth and as You continue to serve us today. We find our contentment and gladness in You. Amen.

Cultivating Heat

Write this letter to the angel of the church in Laodicea. This is the message from the one who is the Amen — the faithful and true witness, the ruler of God's creation: "I know all the things you do, that you are neither hot nor cold. I wish you were one or the other! But since you are like lukewarm water, I will spit you out of my mouth!"
Revelation 3:14-16 NLT

The late F. F. Bosworth, American evangelist and author active in the healing ministry of the late 19th and early to mid-20th century, stated in his book, *Christ the Healer*, "the best thing for us is to be red hot for God. The next best thing is to be cold. But, it is fatal to be lukewarm . . . God says of the man whose heart is hot with love for Him, 'Because he hath set his love upon me, therefore will I deliver him.' "

Lukewarm With a Limp

Hot cereal is meant to be eaten hot, and cold cereal is intended to be eaten cold. Coffee and tea are drunk either hot or icy cold. None of these are pleasurable lukewarm. Neither is a lukewarm Christian's life. A Christian's walk must be uncompromisingly centered on God.

Live *hot* for Christ. Not cold. Not lukewarm with a limp. A lukewarm Christian with a limp:

- Identifies the speck in her sister's eye, yet misses the log in her own eye
- Excuses her own sinful behavior—perhaps thinking she'll be the exception
- Speaks the truth without the necessary element—Love
- Confesses her love for the Lord, but avoids confession and repentance
- Faithfully attends Sunday church, yet forgets what she heard

Jesus Brings the Heat

As portrayed in Scripture, Jesus was kind, compassionate, long-suffering, and merciful. Yet, He straightforwardly spoke the truth throughout His earthly walk. No compromise, no hesitation, no beating around the bush—motivated always by love:

- When the scribes and Pharisees condemned the woman caught in adultery in John 8:7b, Jesus contradicted their dictate saying, *"He who is without sin among you, let him throw a stone at her first."*
- When Jesus faced the woman caught in adultery in John 8:11b, He comforted and commanded her, *"Neither do I condemn you; go and sin no more."*
- When the moneychangers in the Temple in Matthew 21:13 conducted unscrupulous business practices, Jesus confronted them and said, *"It is written, 'My house shall be called a house of prayer,' but you have made it a 'den of thieves.'"*

48

- When Jesus prepared to heal the man at the Pool of Bethesda in John 5:8b, He charged him, *"Rise, take up your bed and walk."*
- When the Samaritan woman in need of Living Water met Jesus at the well in John 4:17b-18, He confronted her affirming, *"You have well said, 'I have no husband,' for you have had five husbands, and the one whom you now have is not your husband; in that you spoke truly."*
- When Jesus spoke to His disciples in John 14:15, He instructed them and all believers who would follow, *"If you love Me, keep My commandments."*

When I compromise the heat of God's Word and His ways in my walk as a Christian by trying to please people at the expense of offending God, I walk with a limp. When we as believers neglect to represent Christ or work for Him while on earth, it is half-hearted and indifferent resulting in compromise. If we grow self-sufficient with no voice or stand for the things of God, we wobble. This is a precarious lukewarm position.

Let's commit to devote ourselves to an all-in relationship with Jesus. Heaven is counting on us and hopeful of us to walk with passion for Christ. God's Kingdom is depending on us to renounce the limp. Lean hard on God, forsake lukewarm, and walk straight, tall, and *hot*.

Consider:
Do you find yourself hot, cold, or lukewarm? If lukewarm, how can you know that God has more for you? What must you do to cultivate a spirit hot for Jesus in your life?

Further Reading:
Lukewarm disposition of Church in Laodicea—Revelation 3:14-22

Prayer:
Father, as I look to You as my loving Savior, may I not be found wanting and lukewarm, but rather wholehearted and committed to You. Thank You for enlightening me using Your Word to point me in the way of life. Amen.

Cultivating an Eternal Life with Jesus

But whenever someone turns to the Lord, the veil is taken away.
For the Lord is the Spirit, and wherever the Spirit of the Lord is,
there is freedom. So all of us who have had that veil removed can
see and reflect the glory of the Lord. And the Lord—who is the
Spirit—makes us more and more like him
as we are changed into his glorious image.
2 Corinthians 3:16-18 NLT

Is Jesus' love for you enough? Is His love for you greater than your strong will?

Have you felt the tug upon your heart? His drawing you to Himself?

He stands at the door of our soul and knocks. He waits for us to open it and allow Him entry into our heart and every area of our lives—to save us, love us, heal us, and restore us unto Himself.

You and I are different in countless ways, yet we are the same in one fundamental way: we both need a Savior. We cannot save ourselves. The chasm of sin that separates mankind from God becomes our demise if we do not accept His beautiful Gift of Salvation—Jesus Christ.

I felt this wooing when I was a young woman aware that there was a void in my innermost being. I felt incomplete but wanted wholeness. When I finally submitted to God's invitation of everlasting life, I prayed with a trusted friend, and by faith, Jesus Christ came into my life to inhabit me and become my Heavenly Father and Savior. I instantly felt a sense of peace. And this was just the beginning of a fulfilling life!

If you are ready to do the same thing to become the complete person you were meant to be, you first need to acknowledge several things:

1. Admit you are a sinner who needs a Savior. You may think you're good enough, like I did with my self-righteous mindset, but none of us can be good enough. This is a deceptive, self-righteous notion. Our sinful nature occurs as a result of the sinfulness of Adam and Eve in the Garden of Eden as recorded in Chapter 3 of the Book of Genesis. You must be willing to humble yourself in the sight of God, your Creator, confessing and forsaking your sins. He does not control or coerce you. The choice is yours and you will need to do this of your own free will.

2. You must realize salvation cannot be earned. It is not based on performing good works. Becoming a Christian—a Christ-follower—is not a religion or just a moral way of life. It is a real, living relationship with our real Living God and Creator.

3. You must acknowledge the penalty of death for your sin must be paid in full. Jesus Christ—God Himself, made flesh, who lived among us 2000 years ago—is the only one who could have done this. On His own terms of redemption, He was the sinless Sacrifice,

risen from death to new life for all time and every soul.

4. Accept Jesus into your heart by faith. Receive Him as your Savior and Lord. He works with you to mold your desires to His perfect will for you. Through the process called sanctification, you will change as you grow spiritually in deeper knowledge and communion with Him.

5. Pray a simple prayer to open yourself to this New Life in Jesus. He is the only way to the Father, the power of the Holy Spirit in every sphere of your life, and to eternal life in Heaven:

Dear God, I acknowledge I am a sinner and cannot save myself. Please forgive me for my sins and all the wrong in my life in thought and deed. Doing good works are important, but they do not secure my eternal salvation with You. Only Jesus can forgive me of my sins because He paid the penalty for them when He died on the cross on my behalf. He secured New Life for me when He rose from the dead. I humble myself before You now and receive You into my heart, by faith, to be my Savior. I submit myself to You as Lord of my life and the teaching ministry of the Holy Spirit as Your disciple. Thank You for coming into my life and hearing my prayer. In the Name of Jesus. Amen.

If by faith you received Jesus as your Savior and Lord, it is the most important decision you have made or ever will make. Please tell a trusted loved one, good friend, or pastor about your decision to receive and follow Christ. Receiving mentoring as you learn about the Bible and doing life God's way will be a process as you grow in God's grace. This is the beginning of a new way of doing life—you will be on your way to fulfilling a destined adventure with Jesus!

Consider:
Who will you contact today to share the good news that you welcomed Jesus into your heart? Ask that person how you can begin to grasp living God's way. If you don't have a Bible, ask your trusted friend for one or buy one. It is a must-have in your walk with the Lord. His Word is His love-letter to you and your handbook to begin to understand all things about living a faith-filled life in Him.

Further Reading:
Our good deeds do not save us—Isaiah 57:12
Accept Jesus as your Savior—John 1:12
All have sinned—Romans 3:23
Salvation is not based on good works—Ephesians 2:8-9
Jesus took our sins on Himself on the cross—1 Peter 2:24
The door of our heart—Revelation 3:20

Prayer:
Dear Jesus, thank You for removing the veil that spiritually separated us, and for coming into my heart by faith today to become my Savior. I will need Your help to live this new life, so help me to do this. Bring new friends and mentors into my life to help me grow in my faith. With new joy and thanksgiving, amen.

WATER

The refreshment
of spiritual virtues
poured into our hungry lives
to help us grow.

Cultivating Faith that Speaks Life

You will also declare a thing, And it will be established for you;
So light will shine on your ways.
Job 22:28 NKJV

Our love for fresh figs birthed when my husband and I were introduced to them while stationed in Italy many decades ago. The fig trees, plentiful there, showcased themselves in the yard of our living quarters and we found them regularly for sale at the neighborhood marketplaces. Deep purple, plump, tender, sweet and juicy—such a delicacy!

Years later, on our property in New Jersey, my husband planted two fig trees. He regularly pruned the bushes to foster their booming growth, and this past year the trees grew to their greatest height with many hundreds of figs on each tree.

Unlike other years, these fruits blossomed early in the summer—yielding a small number for a week or two, and then—suddenly stopped. They brimmed with hard, green fruits, but nothing ripened. I examined the bushes once in a while in June and July, but nothing changed. In early August I visited the bushes hoping to find a ripe fig or two to share with my family, but there still were none. What was taking so long?

I felt a prompt of the Spirit to speak over the trees and proclaim life into them. I told the trees to thrive, to live, and to produce. I thanked God, and then went inside the house, thinking no more about them and not telling anyone I'd prayed over them.

Four days later, I returned home from work to discover a small bowl of deep purple, fully ripened figs on the kitchen counter. My husband had harvested them! We were delighted and thoroughly enjoyed each sweet bite.

The following day a larger bowl of figs was gathered—and the next day. And the next day—more and more figs! Every day we gleaned more abundance of the fruit—we eat them, bake with them, and give bags of them away. Why, as of this writing, we're up to our ears in this fruit!

No one heard my prayer and declaration of life over the fig trees but God. I marvel at how He heard my prayer and answered it beyond my imagining. How much more God cares for us, cares about our cries and major affairs of our lives. The truth reminds me to boldly speak and proclaim Scriptural promises over all our life situations—physical needs, emotional anguish, relational challenges, financial commitments, and national distresses.

In praying as I did, I cultivated my faith speaking over the labor and fruit of my husband's hands. Here are several important take-aways as we proclaim and decree God's promises aloud:

- Release faith using spoken words.
- Speak aloud over personal affairs of life based on Scriptural promises.

- Take hold and ownership of what rightfully belongs to you through consistent prayer and declaration to enforce God's promises fulfilled.
- Following believing prayer or proclamation, take no thought about it—do not worry.
- Thank God for His goodness, grace, and generosity and give Him all the glory.

Consider:

What kinds of situations in your life do you want to believe God for according to His established promises? Contemplate these things, speak them forth in prayer, decree them aloud by faith, and thank God for the manifestation of answered prayer. Journal the outcomes.

Further Reading:

Purposefully listen to and for the Lord—Psalm 85:8

Prayer:

Father, as I declare Your promises into the situations of my life, may my faith mix with Your truth and supernatural power to establish the outcomes. Thank You. Amen.

Cultivating a Glad Heart

All the days of the desponding and afflicted are made evil [by anxious thoughts and forebodings], but he who has a glad heart has a continual feast [regardless of circumstances].
Proverb 15:15 AMP

In the early days of the 2020 pandemic scare event, people were tempted to live their days despondent and afflicted, entertaining anxious thoughts and forebodings.

One day, my friend called me on the phone several days after we'd visited together in the spring. With a slight tremor in her voice, she told me she and her daughter tested positive for the virus. I sensed her uneasiness at the diagnosis. She admitted she didn't have any symptoms to speak of, but her daughter showed some signs including the loss of her sense of taste and smell.

"I just wanted you to know, since you dropped by the other day," she said.

"Yes." I thanked her for the call and thought about our recent visit—without the recommended six-foot distance between us. I had been nursing a slight cough a couple of weeks before, too. According to the experts, the responsible thing would be to get tested, especially since I worked at a school.

I made the required call for a testing appointment and arrived at the doctor's office unalarmed. I entertained a split second of concern over the unpleasantness of the test itself and when the nurse asked, "Were you wearing masks?"

Gulp. No.

That evening, the testing site called with the results—negative. I was glad to hear it. Would I have been as glad if it had been positive?

For my part, when in the presence of someone who sneezed, I didn't worry with anxious thoughts of, *What if I caught the virus?* I felt no anxiety when I chose not to wear my mask in the car or outside when I left the house. My mind did not swirl with the worst-case scenario of infection that daily news briefings promised were inevitable.

Instead of peace from a glad heart, there were many caught up in a cloud of foreboding, in isolation until "the experts," with their ever changing analysis, said it was safe. Should worry steal our gladness?

Anxious thoughts assail both mind and heart and trigger negative emotions. But research proves approximately 85% of worrisome thoughts never materialize. Time spent nursing worry and anxiety can never be retrieved from last year or last night. Wasted moments of fear and foreboding, that could have been better used, are gone forever.

How can we fortify ourselves against the temptation to worry and its despondent byproduct in the daily practice of cultivating a glad heart?

One way I cultivate gladness is to recall my blessings and little pleasures. I view many things in my life with appreciation including my morning cup of Twining English Breakfast Tea—Bold. It has a rich, robust flavor that welcomes me into a new day. I sip it from my favorite mug, steaming hot and aromatic. It's a morning satisfaction I cherish as I sit in my quiet-time chair. Taking joy in a daily teatime seems like a small thing, but it grows in value when I view it with gladness—health to my soul and spirit.

Another way I practice glad-heartedness is when I regard a simple task as significant. I turn ordinary activities into out of the ordinary experiences. For example, when I go to the grocery store, I enjoy choosing healthy foods and remain observant for people God may place in my path who need help. Perhaps they can use a coupon I have stashed in my purse, or there may be an opportunity to share a tract with a stranger in the parking lot. These simple jaunts often result in encounters that gladden my heart.

On excursions, when my husband drives us to the shore, an out-of-town mall, or the airport, I take books with me—usually several books. I have no problem reading in a moving car and make good use of travel time with a book or conversation with my husband. I consider how pleasant it is to enjoy our date time. I notice the lovely weather and reflect on the freedom I have to take an outing—to just appreciate these moments.

Keep a record of your ordinary glad moments in a journal. I have a stack of six completed journals and am currently filling up the seventh. What do I write about? I keep notes from my pastor's sermons, inspirations the Lord whispers to my heart, answers to prayer, and notes from internet teachings to later review or share with others. These snippets of my life reflect who I am deep within my heart and what's important to me.

Sound simple? Sometimes the most basic joys from the Lord gladden the heart best. Cultivate simplicity in your life and you will discover much to be glad about. When we trust God regardless of circumstances—good or ill—we learn to lean on Him, and actively resist the worrisome assaults of the devil.

If the fearful judgments from the 2020 virus predictions alarmed you and caught you by surprise, take joy in the glad fact you survived to read these words. For this, I am so thankful—and glad for you.

During the difficult days of the 2020 pandemic, as many experienced physical challenges, financial adversities, and disconnections or loss with loved ones and friends, people have survived relatively unscathed. Live forward, knowing life holds troublesome seasons that can never trounce a soul steadfast in Christ, cultivated in the goodness of God with a glad heart.

Consider:

In what ways do you cultivate and express a glad heart? Have you ever shared these ideas with others? If so, what did that conversation sound like?

Prayer:

Father, when anxiety and thoughts of foreboding tempt me to feel despondent, may Your presence gladden my heart and change my mind to focus on You. Help me to cultivate gladness in the simple blessings You shower upon me—a daily feast as I trust You through every circumstance. Amen.

Author's Note: Within this message, I do not seek to diminish any of my readers' grief or pain suffered if a loved one did not survive the effects of this ominous virus. Please know I sincerely care and desire you to read this devotional, discovering a new hope to propel you forward.

Cultivating a Merciful Heart

Blessed be the God and Father of our Lord Jesus Christ, the
Father of mercies and God of all comfort . . .
2 Corinthians 1:3 ESV

Make much of God's mercy. It's a gift. A colossal gift.

As I review the many Scriptural examples of God's mercy, I'm compelled while challenged to mirror His merciful character. Reflecting on the numerous accounts of His mercy toward me in my life, I rely on His grace to help me cultivate a merciful heart.

God's mercy is chock-full of compassion. It's like a get-out-of-jail free ticket. As a youngster, when I played the board game Monopoly™, if I'd been sent to jail and drew a get-out-of-jail free card, I sighed in relief. My release was freely granted—no fine, no longer sentenced to serve time in Monopoly™ jail, no further postponement. Pass GO and collect $200.

Growing up in a large city in New York I recall many instances of God's mercy. It was a normal and natural thing to routinely play outside. I rode my bike to friends' homes and walked to the local park, zoo, swimming pool, bowling alley, and ice-skating rink. My siblings and I trekked through snow to reach hills on which to sled and toboggan

My friends and I played badminton, kick ball, and dodge ball for countless hours on my street. Normal and natural. I survived all of these adventures with a few minor scrapes on my knees and ankle, but nothing serious. God's faithful mercy.

As a high-schooler, I rode a city bus to school and occasionally walked home alone at the end of the day—approximately two miles—as I participated in after-school sports. On certain days, I worked at a grocery store after school from 5:00pm to 9:00pm. It wasn't far from home, but because my father worked evenings and my mom didn't drive, I walked home alone. After dark, my mom would meet me half-way, but the thought of passing by a huge, abandoned factory on a house-less stretch of road felt unsettling. My uneasiness diminished when I spotted Mom. In hindsight, I recognize the merciful protection granted me from a God I didn't yet know personally.

God was there in the dark, and He was there when I felt alone.

Our lives overflow with God's mercies. Lamentations 3 affirms His mercies are fresh every morning and thankfully so, because we need them with each new day. They restore us and provide us with another opportunity and renewed expectation.

The comforting and compassionate heart of God is expressed in James 2 affirming mercy triumphs over judgment. Jesus was perfect in His judgments—not blind to humanity's sinfulness. Nevertheless, in His divine understanding He illustrated mercy using powerful examples to showcase agape love. He knew we would desperately need to adopt it.

- Jesus chose mercy with the woman caught in the act of adultery. The hypocritical men in their accusatory tones felt she should be stoned. Instead of asking, *How could you be so immoral?* Jesus told her He didn't condemn her; she was to leave and sin no more.
- Jesus chose mercy when He fed the multitudes. Instead of lecturing the masses, *Why were you neglectful to bring your own food?* Jesus directed the apostles to feed them, and He then miraculously increased the fare to feed five thousand.
- Jesus chose mercy when He ministered deliverance and healing to great crowds. Instead of questioning, *What did you do to invite this disease or foul spirit into your body?* Jesus liberated and healed them all.

To offer encouragement, the New Living Translation footnote from Ephesians 4:32 explains, ". . . God forgives us, not because we forgive others, but solely because of his great mercy. As we come to understand his mercy, however, we will want to be like him." Mercy positions itself next to forgiveness and kindness.

We become more Christlike when we cultivate a merciful way of life. Let's respond and remember to:
- Begin with the desire and a decision to be merciful
- Attend to Jesus' examples of merciful behavior
- Recall the countless instances God bestows mercy to us
- Grow in Christlikeness granting mercy to others

Appreciate today how God's mercies are present in your life and your family's. Contemplate with a grateful heart as you make much of His mercies.

Consider:
Explain how God's been available for you when you desperately needed His mercy and lovingkindness. As you've come to understand the mercy of God, in what ways have you discovered you want to be more like Him? How has His mercy toward you propelled you to be more merciful?

Further Reading:
Mercy persists forever—Psalm 107:1
The Lord is kind and merciful—Psalm 145:8
Steadfast love and daily mercies—Lamentations 3:22-23
Love mercy—Micah 6:6-8
Those who are merciful will receive mercy—Matthew 5:7
Woman caught in adultery—John 8
Jesus fed multitudes—Luke 9
Jesus ministered to masses—Luke 6

Prayer:
Father, Your everyday mercies and constant comfort display Your steadfast care for me. May I be prompt to extend mercy to others as a faithful reflection of You. Amen.

Cultivating Prevailing Love

Long ago the Lord said to Israel:
'I have loved you, my people, with an everlasting love.
With unfailing love I have drawn you to myself.'
Jeremiah 31:3 NLT

I met a Christian woman while doing some volunteer work some years ago. We became friends but weren't close companions—didn't go to lunch or hang together. We were sisters-in-Christ, but I felt a disconnect with her and sensed she didn't care much for me. I wrestled in my heart: *Why doesn't she like me?* An awkward unrest inflated inside me.

As the inner tension grew, so did my frustration. When I couldn't tolerate how this consumed me, I approached God with my angst and irritation. By this time, I was in sin regarding my ill feelings towards her and sensed God's conviction prod me. It felt like a strong, uncomfortable nagging in my inner man.

Conviction is God's way of showing us we're off track and headed in a dead-end direction. The only way to relieve this severe, unsettling pressure is to get back on track with God and yield to Him with a repentant attitude. This is the turning point where God receives and relieves the pressure and says, *That's the way, My dear child. Instead of resisting Me by running away in your own direction, run toward Me. I'll exchange your sin for My righteousness and peace. I've already accomplished this for you at the cross.*

In prayer, I confessed my sin to God, and felt an inaudible impression to begin praying for her. I didn't expect to hear this, and I didn't want to do it. I continued to sense His prompting: *Pray for her and do whatever you can to be pleasant, helpful, and loving.*

As I agreed to God's remedy and direction, He changed my heart. The pressure lifted and I knew I was forgiven and cleansed with words of direction and encouragement, *You can do this — now do it My way. Esteem her with My never-ending love and ability that are already within you.* God responds to a contrite and humbled attitude and heart. Although this friend moved away, when I occasionally connect with her via facetime and email, I get excited! It's not only been a decision to pray for and love her, I feel God's love overflowing towards her inside me. I'm eager to catch up with her in conversation and with written communication.

The Lord is the reason we can love so extravagantly. This is agape love — God's perfect and sacrificial love. It's placed in our hearts by the Holy Spirit when He comes to indwell us.

If you find you're struggling to love someone or even yourself, give God permission to move around in your heart. Imagine your heart as a home — invite Him to walk around and enter all the rooms in the house. You may feel hesitant to allow Him into some areas because you may be hiding secrets in that room, or a closet may be too cluttered or soiled with your messes — sins — including bitterness, resentment, or unfinished business. If you humbly invite Him in, you'll recognize His voice prompting you, *I've been waiting for this moment. I can help you with the clutter and the messes—just give them all to Me. I'm more than elated and willing to help you. I'll lift this burden and heavy weight from you.*

In our opening Scripture, the Lord is speaking to Israel. But His divine message of love and restoration in this verse includes all people who dare to trust Him. God faithfully outstretches His love and arms toward His people with affection and kind-heartedness. As James 4 reminds us, when we draw near to God with humility, He'll faithfully draw near to us.

Consider:
How would you describe to a loyal friend or spouse about a fractured or estranged relationship you have with someone? If you're willing to cultivate prevailing love, will you consider meeting with God in prayer to speak and listen to Him about it? If so, please don't hesitate any longer. He's been waiting for this moment.

Further Reading:
My yoke is easy, and My burden is light—Matthew 11:30
God's love poured into our hearts by the Holy Spirit—Romans 5:5
Draw near to God—James 4:8a

Prayer:
Father, there's no truer love than Yours, an everlasting love. I've learned to draw close to You and realize the security and authenticity You provide. As I'm Your beloved child, You'll never turn me away. Thank You. Amen.

Cultivating Holy Prompts

My sheep hear my voice, and I know them, and they follow me.
John 10:27 ESV

Have you ever felt you were supposed to get your hair done at a *certain* salon or shop at a *particular* store or call someone at a *defined* time? These promptings can often result in divine appointments.

I like the way my stylist cuts my hair. She's gifted and graciously accommodating. I enjoy the connection God fashions as we talk and share with each other. These encounters have become more than appointments for a new do, but God-appointed connections to share God-ordained dreams for future days and God-manifested dreams already realized. We're both Holy Spirit energized.

Follow the holy risk. If you are a Christian, then God's Spirit dwells in your heart. Ordinary actions can result in extraordinary results when we follow the sacred prod. The revealed exhortation in Isaiah 48:17 ESV is "Thus says the Lord, your Redeemer, the Holy One of Israel: 'I am the Lord your God, who teaches you to profit, who leads you in the way you should go.'"

I've come to expect God to be in my daily encounters. Why wouldn't I—He's my loving Father! So, if you ever feel led to pray a prayer, write and send a cheery note, or call/text a loved one or friend, do it. It can result in a forever moment—blessing an individual and glorifying God!

Consider:

If you have felt a nudge to do a certain thing, go to a specific place, or pray an urgent prayer, what was your response? Think of the times you followed that nudge, and perhaps times you failed to do so. What were the consequences? Describe them.

Prayer:

Father, as I lean on You, may You count on me to learn to hear Your voice and follow Your holy prompts. Amen.

Cultivating I AM

God said to Moses, "I AM who I AM." And he said, "Say this to the people of Israel: 'I AM has sent me to you.' "
Exodus 3:14 ESV

In Exodus 3, Scripture explains God is the I AM—the mighty God who always has been and who will never change. I AM is His name forever; He is to be remembered throughout all generations.

In John 8, Jesus maintains His infinite existence stating He existed before Abraham was even born–the eternal I AM. He stands present to forever reside with His people and to deliver them.

Because by faith I AM lives within me and will inhabit all others who embrace Him, He makes it possible for you and me to exist and persevere as an *I Can* woman.

To cultivate life as an *I Can* woman we say:
- I can do all things
- I can go forward
- I can face tomorrow . . . and today
- I can do what seems impossible

I Can Do All Things
Is this the change I heard about?!

Post-menopausal years proved a challenge to me as my body experienced changes such as my sleep patterns shifting.

I coupled seeking God for help with natural-healing answers to this new season. Although I'm no longer a spring-chicken with the spryness of a 20-something, I'm adjusting better these days—especially since I'm leaning on and resting more peacefully in Christ.

The Lord impressed upon me to give Him the angst I experienced and to trust Him with these changes. To offer Him a sacrifice of praise and a sacrifice of joy. I expected that my trial would result in multiple freedoms for me. If you are going through a similar season right now, lean into the I AM. It is the only way you can.

Philippians 4:13 offers encouragement that with the help of Christ who gives me necessary strength for the day at hand, I can do all things–even the very hard things in life. Therefore, I can get out of bed, accomplish God-given goals, show up for work on scheduled days, rest in His faithful love and promises—and write books!

I Can Go Forward

It felt daunting. At the age of 54, I embarked upon a master's program of study. For decades I was interested in and informally read about relational and emotional health. The dream incubated in my spirit for five years before I took the first steps to enroll as a graduate student at Liberty University. Planting the first step is oftentimes the toughest.

A partial scholarship opened up for me, and my husband and I agreed I was to walk forward to begin this new journey. As I prepared to register, I felt the still small whisper in my heart, *It's now or never.* There was an urgency in my soul that I had come to a crossroad I wouldn't see again. In God's determined timing, I pressed forward and accomplished this God-planted dream.

I Can Face Tomorrow . . . and Today

It was a process, but my heart ultimately found repose, hope, and expectation in God as I navigated through the empty-nest season. The intimate message from Psalm 62:5 makes it possible to face every day—to wait solely upon God and soundlessly yield to Him as my expectation arises from Him.

Gradual loss of relational dynamics occurs when children become teens and young adults. They spend less time together with their parents, they develop their own schedules, their standards and beliefs solidify, and they don't seek parental advice as frequently. They are preparing to leave the nest which is a normal and natural phase of their development.

I laid down a sense of empty nest loss that hampered me and embraced the truth that relationships with our children don't end when they reach adulthood. They develop into beloved friends and often confidantes. As we allow this process to unfold healthily, we're able to brave each day and cultivate expectant hearts.

I Can Do What Seems Impossible

You don't want to drive that stretch of notorious highway! Hearing other people share their trepidation when driving certain Philadelphia highways struck fear in my own thinking and heart as I came to believe I couldn't drive this treacherous span of road alone. But when my father became critically ill and I needed to drive to upstate New York using this route to reach him, I found I could do so when I prayed, took authority over the spirit of fear in Jesus' Name, and applied action by tackling the drive alone. Doing what I thought I couldn't do by just doing it.

Eureka! I began to look forward to driving this highway. I could hardly wait! I rolled down the car windows, cranked up my music, and picked up the pace to join the race with the rest of the speedsters. Fear moved out, kicked to the side of the road, while Faith and Courage joined me on the passenger side.

Jesus explained in Luke 1:37 that nothing is impossible with God. What once seemed impossible for many years—me, alone, navigating a challenging highway—was now made possible with God.

Because of I AM, you can. You're just a decision away—step forward to do the things your heart prompts, face tough but feasible feats, and witness the seemingly impossible manifest.

Consider:
What challenges are you withstanding in your life that can become victory-stories when you recognize I AM is in you to make you an I Can woman of God? What are you waiting for? He's for you and will meet you. What changes are you willing to make to grow in your faith as you identify these challenges?

Further Reading:
The I AM presents Himself to deliver—Exodus 3
In the beginning was God—John 1
The I AM before Abraham—John 8
Sacrifice of joy—Psalm 27
Still small voice; holy prompts—1 Kings 19:12
All things are possible with God—Matthew 19:26

It was for freedom that Christ set us free—Galations 5:1

Prayer:

Father, it's awesome to realize You dwell within us as the great I AM. Thank You for enabling us to live with grace and Your presence to overcome even the very demanding situations in life. Amen.

Cultivating Honesty Before the Lord

The woman said to him, "Sir, I perceive that you are a prophet."
John 4:19 ESV

She didn't reveal her honest self to Him. But Jesus knew her. All about her. The woman at the well.

John 4:1-26 relates the story of a Samaritan woman, identified in her town as one who lived a sordid lifestyle, arriving at the well for water to satisfy her thirst—a short-term need. Accustomed to being used and rejected, she was surprised to meet Jesus, who requested a drink from her.

"I am both a Samaritan and a woman. You are a Jew. Why do you speak to me?"

But Jesus did speak to her. He engaged her in conversation with curious questions and more curious answers, then offered her Living Water—a gift from God able to quench a lifetime of eternal need.

Believing Jesus to be a prophet, she questioned Him about the correct place to worship. Jesus responded, "The physical place of worship will no longer be important. True worshippers glorify God in reverence and in truth."

Jesus revealed Himself to be the Messiah, the One in whom she had placed her expectation even though she had lived in sin. But she was not convinced.

"Go then," Jesus said, "and get your husband."

She replied, "I have no husband."

Jesus pressed her with truth and straightforwardly acknowledged, "You're correct that you have no husband. In fact, you've had five husbands and aren't married to the current man with whom you live."

The Living Word pierced her spirit. *Surely this man is the Messiah. He has told me all about me!* The woman abandoned her waterpot and ran to the town to testify to everyone she met about Jesus revealing Himself to her at the well. Many believed in Jesus due to her testimony and His Word.

She must have marveled in her heart, *Could this be the kind of love and freedom I've craved for my whole life?!*

Just as Jesus understood all about the Samaritan woman's life, He knows all about our lives, too. The woman at the well never told Him anything about herself. But He knew all about her, nonetheless. He told her what she would not tell Him and offered her a better way to live while speaking honestly to her, with love, about her sinful lifestyle.

How about you? Are you like the woman at the well, trying to hide shameful episodes of your life from Jesus? Cultivate honesty before the Lord because He already knows all things about you—and loves you fully. Stop trying to face life alone behind a mask. Be honest about yourself before Him. Give your brokenness, disappointments, and sadness of heart to the Lord. Live blessed because:

Jesus knows your . . .
- Fears, faults, failures
- Guilt, grief, guile

- Pain, past, pride
- Shame, sin
- Sorrow, struggles
- Temper, torment, temptations

He also knows your . . .
- Desires
- Dreams
- Future
- Growth
- Heart
- Value
- Victories
- Worth

Nothing surprises the Lord. Let Him sever the shackles that bind you, so you are free to pick up the hope and possibilities He has prepared for you. Then do as the late Elizabeth Elliot said: "Leave it all in the Hands that were wounded for you."

Consider:
Identify and journal about the areas in your heart where brokenness or disappointment may hide and reside. Take courage and submit them to the Lord in a written prayer. God yearns to meet with you!

Further Reading:
The Samaritans' change of heart—John 4:1-42
Living water—John 7:37-39

Prayer:

Father, understanding who You are, I choose to take my strength from You. I unmask myself to approach You in all truth and honesty—for a closer relationship built on authenticity. Amen.

Cultivating Contentment

But godliness with contentment is great gain.
1 Timothy 6:6 ESV

Frustration—we all get frustrated. The root of frustration is fear resulting in impatience, anxiety, and annoyance. We think, *This isn't fair and I'm not getting what I think I should* or *Will I ever get what I want?!*

James 4 describes frustration in prayer when we don't get what we want or, with faulty ambitions, desire what others have. Frustration upends contentment in our life.

To safeguard and cultivate contentment in our relationship, my husband and I declare a helpful phrase when we become impatient or frustrated with the other: *Remember, we're not each other's enemy.*

In other words, we have an enemy, Satan, who seeks to disrupt our unity, peace, and satisfaction with each other. We may need to iron out some differences of opinion or perspective using explanation and respectful conversation, but we allow God to work in our hearts and in our marital relationship. Peace, contentment, and satisfaction replace unrest, impatience, and frustration.

When my husband and I feel frustrated or distressed, we confront it and seek to restore our hearts to a place of contentment. While we want to address frustration, we don't want to murmur, brood or gossip. 1 Corinthians 10:9-10 reminds us not to grumble or complain as these are displeasing to God, putting Him to the test as some Old Testament Israelites did.

Once, during a challenging situation, the Holy Spirit whispered to my spirit, *How long are you going to be frustrated with this man? You know you're eventually going to come around, so why not get over it sooner rather than later?* God's divine wisdom. Smile.

We also resist stuffing irritations down in our heart and isolating ourselves. Since everyone faces frustrations, three biblical practices apply to help us cultivate godly contentedness:

Walk in the Spirit of God

When we move in step with the Spirit of God, Galatians 5 cites that we don't satisfy or serve the carnal demands of our fleshly-natural inclinations. We yield to the Holy Spirit to make decisions and learn to follow God's love walking in His Spirit.

When we exercise our bodies, we practice and work out strategic maneuvers with a determined end. The exercise and drills become second nature as we perform them again and again. God's love leads us this way as we heed His Spirit to practice and respond in line with Him.

Clothe Ourselves with the Whole Armor of God

In Ephesians 6, the apostle Paul explains how we can be strong in the Lord's mighty power. We brace ourselves daily with God's armor to shield ourselves from the enemy's assaults. We put on—clothe ourselves—with God's force and strength to withstand Satan's schemes against us. Paul explains we do not wrangle with people, but rather against devilish spirits in unseen realms who try to disrupt and harm us. He admonishes us to stand against these evil forces and resist them, outfitted in God's armor, for the Lord is with us to deliver.

Nurture Gratefulness

When we implement a thankful attitude daily, it nourishes our entire being. Adopting a grateful perspective and outlook as our orientation to life results in physical, spiritual, and emotional wholeness and hallmark contentment. When practicing gratitude, I cushion myself from stress, enhance my immune system, and produce more ease to help me relax and rest quietly. Repeatedly the Scripture exhorts us to maintain thankfulness in our deliberate meditations. As we do this, it cultivates satisfaction and contentment, fostering great gain.

Because frustration is inevitable, we do well to control it using God's methods. Walk in the Holy Spirit, dressed in the Armor of God with a thankful perspective. This yields a contented life filled with the benefits of God's promises. As we cultivate godliness with satisfaction and contentment in our personal lives and within our relationships, we obtain significant advantages.

Consider:

What ways do you quench frustrations and discontent in your life? What healthy changes can you make today to cultivate the great gain referred to in the above Scripture?

Further Reading:

Selfish desires at war within us—James 4:1-3
Walk in God's Spirit—Galatians 5:16-17

Whole Armor of God—Ephesians 6:10-18
Thankfulness—Ephesians 5:20, Philippians 4:6, Colossians 3:17

Prayer:
Father, I choose contentment and satisfaction as I walk in Your Spirit to glorify You and to harmonize my relationships. I am personally fulfilled when I espouse godliness with contentment. Thank You, Lord, for helping to make this possible. Amen.

Cultivating Peace on Stormy Seas

*Let not your hearts be troubled. Believe in God; believe also in
me. In my Father's house are many rooms. If it were not so,
would I have told you that I go to prepare a place for you?
. . . Peace I leave with you; my peace I give to you. Not as the
world gives do I give to you. Let not your hearts be troubled,
neither let them be afraid.*
John 14:1-2, 27 ESV

Do you know what it's like to be on a boat tossed
uncontrollably by waves and wind on a stormy sea?
Unguarded, a fierce storm creeps upon you as worry and
fear venture to strike.

As a newlywed, my husband and I were invited on a
large boat for a fishing party in the bay off the New Jersey
coastline. The day trip confined me on the deck of a boat
with a group of new acquaintances—my first foray into
flounder fishing.

I had no time to think about cleaning and eating the
fish for dinner later once tumultuous waves tossed the
vessel and overwhelmed me. Jittery and apprehensive with
each choppy splash of foamy, salty water against the side of
the boat, my composure collapsed, and my perception of
control ebbed. I felt outside my comfort zone and
vulnerable.

The fishy scent nauseated me, and a quivering queasiness struck my stomach unabated. An unbalanced step replaced my land-lubber sure-footedness. My cheery disposition vanished as my skin crawled with a clutching clamminess I'd never felt before. I upchucked every morsel of food in my stomach overboard and nearly lost my glasses with it! The captain escorted me into the dark cabin of the boat, and I laid flat for the remainder of the day—settled to some degree, feeling awkward among strangers and eager for rescue.

Though the sun shone bright overhead and the others on board seemed to enjoy the outing, every sway of the boat felt like a choppy storm at sea to me.

Stormy seas were not new to the disciples—many of whom made their living on the water. It was a common trial of life all fishermen had experienced. Like the day a storm tossed their boat with Jesus at rest, fast asleep at the back of the boat, as told in Mark 4:36-39.

While the disciples were panic-stricken as water burst over the sides of their boat and flooded the deck, they awakened Jesus with a clamor of alarm. They couldn't understand how he could sleep so soundly in such a dangerous storm.

Jesus awoke and addressed the circumstances—wind and water—to be stilled. And the storm ceased. He then queried the disciples about their fear even though He was among them. They didn't look to Jesus as their example in the storm but imposed their faithless response upon Him instead.

How often do we underestimate Jesus' power and presence in our storms when we're panicked?

Remember Jesus' example and wise instructions to the disciples when stormy seas of trials toss you. His assurance of empowerment for supernatural peace is clear:

- Take authority over invasive circumstances
- Guard your heart when trouble strikes
- Have faith—believe and trust God

To me, peace is a place of comfort. A safe place where I feel whole in my entire being—spirit, body, and mind. I feel God's peace when the lights are dimmed, doors are locked, a supple blanket swaddles me, and sweet-tempered air, with a hint of fragrant florals, surrounds me. Not too cold. Not too hot. Just right.

A boat rocked by a storm is not a place of comfort, yet Jesus rested at peace as it raged around Him. He knew who His Father was and who He was in His Father. Storms did not confuse Him. He stabilized and steadied Himself, the boat, and his panicked disciples as our Example-Bearer in a moment of trial.

Jesus acknowledged that storms in life would come, but we did not need to be shaken by them. He was in the boat with the disciples—right beside them.

Psalm 16:8 NLT states, "I know the Lord is always with me. I will not be shaken, for He is right beside me."

Life is fraught with storms. But we can be secure resting on Jesus our Rock in the trials that come our way. Be it a tempest of health, relationships, finances, children, careers, or global upheavals, He remains our Example-Bearer, focused on Father God.

Cultivate a focused mind in your stormy seas—single-mindedly locked on Jesus and the peace He provides.

Similar to snapping a photograph—the mama bird feeding her baby, the cheery child able to sit up alone, or the stunning hues of the evening sunset—the lens' focus and attention zeroes in on the one thing I seek to capture. Metaphorically, if I allow distractions to interfere as I focus and steady myself on Jesus, the bird flies away, the child stops smiling, and clouds roll in to blur the night sky. I miss what could have been with my mind and body steady in a posture until the photo is caught. Until the storm passes.

I know the storm will pass. It always passes. Jesus assures me, when my focus becomes my thoughts aligned with God's thoughts, steadied as I hunker down in God, anchored to Him.

Consider:
Describe a personal storm—one you survived but didn't think you would. What means and methods did you use to endure through that time? How did you experience the supernatural peace of Jesus as spoken of in the Scripture? If you struggled to focus on His peace, how can you believe and embrace His gift to help you through your current tempests?

Further Reading:
Jesus is at hand—Philippians 4:5
Rejoice in the Lord always; storm or no storm—Philippians 4:4
Instructions Jesus left His followers—Mark 16:15-18
Jesus is our peace—Ephesians 2:14
My hiding place—Psalm 32:7

Prayer:

Father, thank You for being faithful to deliver me from the confusion and chaos of the stormy seas of life. I can know You as my peace in my past, in my present, and continued peace into my future because You are the same yesterday, today, and forever, and Your words and promises will never pass away. Amen.

Cultivating Peace: What Rocks Your World?

. . . For He has said, "I will never leave you nor forsake you."
Hebrews 13:5b ESV

What is it that unnerves you? What is it that worries you? Do any of these situations rock you off your God-given place of peace?

- Health concerns
- Finances
- Marital relationships
- Issues with children

Rocky Health Terrain

When I encounter health issues that threaten to derail and distract me, the anxiety they create, even as I still grapple with some, threatens to unsettle my heart.

For a number of years, headaches and acid-reflux agitation attempted to steal my focus in life and my joy. Ever notice how the word "attempted" holds within it the word "tempt?" The temptation to doubt, and yield to discouragement and disbelief, reared its ugly head. When I prayed about these concerns, sometimes I didn't hear anything from God. My peace was rocked.

Health woes can cause confusion and disrupt the composure of both soul and mind. We must persevere in prayer. As we trust and wait in Him, He reveals the next steps we ought to take towards relief. This may come in the form of immediate healing or restored wellness over time as we prevail in believing prayer and hold fast to His peace.

I know this to be true. I am headache and acid-reflux free today. Glory to God!

Financial Peaks and Valleys

How about finances? In the early season of our marriage, my husband and I endured financial leanness, living on a constricted budget. When I was newly discharged from the military and began my college experience, I volunteered part-time with a sports program at the Christian school our church sponsored. Approximately a year later, I was offered a position within the school, which included a modest salary, while I pursued my college studies.

My husband encountered several job layoffs throughout the first couple decades of our marriage. He supplemented our income with side self-employment for fifteen years.

We started our family and desired that I be a stay-at-home mom with our children before they entered school. This was the right choice for us, and I loved being there while I continued my pursuit of a college degree part-time. Even so, this delayed our ability to purchase a house for many years before God smoothed a path to home ownership and faithfully sustained us through rocky, uphill years.

The stress of making ends meet with limited resources can morph into a type of idolatry if it monopolizes our thought life and magnifies fear.

Marital Mountains

Whenever two independent people come together in marriage, it doesn't take long to discover their contrasting practices of doing life.

He allows his mail to pile up and she, preferring tidiness and order, desires daily attention to it: toss it, file it, or organize it. This is only one example of numerous ways a couple may differ.

The Bible offers wisdom on this topic in the Song of Solomon 2, which explains how the "little foxes" in a relationship can cause irritation and conflict, often resulting in weighty squabbles. These little foxes rock us if we allow them to cause harsh accusations and arguments. Peace is swapped for self-aggrandizement. It is wise for couples to respectfully discuss these differences and agree to compromise or focus on gratefulness toward each other, the person they call friend, lover, and spouse.

Peace may be sacrificed for a period when the little foxes of delicate differences rise to the surface. Submission to God in such moments allows sanity to return. Healthy discussion alleviates some rocky tension.

Child-rearing Stumbling Stones

Children are Gifts from God—treasures. When we bring them home from the hospital, we observe them closely so we can learn who these little ones are. Proverbs 22:6 teaches us to seek God regarding our children's distinct abilities and talents.

These little people will be influenced by Mommy and Daddy, but will grow as their own individual selves, formed by the unique imprint of God and their parents' vision—or lack of vision—for them. This can be a two-edged sword and may frustrate both parents and children. Parents may try to squeeze their youngsters into a mold that doesn't fit—like forcing a square peg into a round hole. Life rocks and peace shakes.

Do not impose your dreams upon your children. Avoid the self-serving temptation to do so that is motivated apart from God's intended destiny for them. Frederick Buechner said that our calling is ". . . that place where your deepest gladness and the world's deepest hunger meet." Peace will prevail when we encourage and provide opportunities leading them in providential pathways toward their potential calling.

The peace Jesus gives is not based on circumstances such as *"I've received my healing!" "We closed on our first home!" "We booked our long-awaited vacation!" "Our children agreed with our decisions!"*

These are all worthy of celebration, but the elation of the sought-after event will fade. When Jesus is present, no matter the circumstance, peace is present. He stills the soul, quiets the mind, and completes the spirit.

Peace, in the Person of Jesus Christ, abides in our innermost being. He doesn't move in and out like tenants who come and go from a rental property. His Presence is ever present. And is peace.

Often, we must fight to maintain our foothold of peace, a still and quiet soul, due to the enemy's distractions that threaten to rock our world. The peace that Jesus gives is central to our well-being on every peak or rocky terrain we travel in life. Don't scale mountains without Him. Get closer to Jesus. He is at hand.

Consider:

Identify and list the troublesome, rocky road distractions in your life that steal your peace. How have you cultivated peace, navigated harsh terrain, and guarded your peace from being stolen?

Further Reading:

Little foxes—Song of Solomon 2:8-17

Prayer:

Father, when we're plagued with difficulties and trials meddling with our peace, we may feel like we're being consumed, but You are with us to steady the rockiness. May we always trust in Your unfailing arm to rescue us from a rocky world. Amen.

Cultivating Trust in Every Trial

When you go through deep waters, I will be with you . . .
Isaiah 43:2 NLT

Several years ago, I faced a fierce trial. Although it didn't last long, it shook me and tried to dishearten me.

It was a Friday when I disclosed personal information at a prayer conference. Consecrated prayer intercessors were on staff to meet the needs of attendees; all information would remain confidential. The women serving me listened carefully, while the Lord's gifts operated. I felt relieved as I shared what was unnerving me. It felt as if my heart and spirit were unzipped as these caring women seemed to read my undraped soul.

The hurdle arose when, after my prayer session ended, I left the building and suddenly felt undone — unclothed and naked. My thoughts thundered, *What did I just do?*

The next day I regretted my surrender for prayer where I'd divulged private information without closure to my situation. Throughout the entire day, a cloud of oppression and condemnation assaulted me. The enemy whispered lies to me: *You shouldn't have gone; You made a mistake by telling about your anguish; You've made things worse.*

That evening, I determined I would not attend church the following day. I was too distressed and despondent and surely could not face anyone.

But shortly past midnight while asleep in my bed, the Lord's presence visited me. In the dark, I opened my eyes and felt a strong peace surround me. In my mind's eye I discerned Jesus reaching down, deep into the recesses of my heart. Rehabilitating me. Zipping me up. Finalizing what was unfinished in an instant!

I recall smiling in my bed, in the dark, as I recognized God's sacred ministry to me, His daughter. Of course I would attend church in the morning! His peace covered me as the fire of oppression was extinguished and my joy restored. It was a beautiful testimony of God's deliverance when the enemy of my soul, Satan, threatened to dishearten and oppress me.

Sometimes we're delivered in a moment, while sometimes we're delivered after scores of moments. Both types of deliverance confirm God is always with us. The trials may involve finances, health, or relationships. However they are packaged, may we confidently acknowledge we are not alone as Isaiah 43:2 NLT reminds us, *When you go through deep waters, I will be with you. When you go through rivers of difficulty, you will not drown. When you walk through the fire of oppression, you will not be burned up; the flames will not consume you.*

In this passage, there are three different levels of trials. I envision myself in God's loving arms as my heroic rescuer in each of these predicaments:
- The *deep waters* are the minor challenges.
- The *rivers of difficulty* represent the severe conflicts.
- The *fires of oppression* are the most desperate places.

In all of these circumstances, God is faithfully present.

Though we experience valleys with shadows of death and darkness, they are just that—shadows. Moreover, shadows have no power and change with the passage of time and circumstances as they distort perceptions. In Psalm 23:4 ESV, King David trusted in God's grace through such valleys when he stated, "Even though I walk through the valley of the shadow of death, I will fear no evil, for you are with me; your rod and staff, they comfort me."

Stand fast and know that, however deliverance occurs—whether sooner or later, God is with us. Through it all, rejoice and maintain a heart and posture of joy because, as Nehemiah 8:8-10 reminds us, the joy of the Lord is our lifeline and strength.

If we let them, our trials can work *for* us because of God's faithful love towards us. He promises to deliver us from evil because the Kingdom, power, and glory belong to Him. This serves to bolster us in mind and spirit to become more Christlike, trusting Him, as He forms our character in deep waters, rivers, and fires.

Consider:

How have you experienced trials on all three of the levels mentioned above? How do you behave through your varied plights? Identify some of the ways God has shown Himself strong to you through your challenges.

Further Reading:

Trials lead to endurance and strength of character—Romans 5:3-5

The Lord rejoices over us with song and quiets us with His love—Zephaniah 3:17

Prayer:
Father, may I recognize that I am not alone in my trials, they are temporary, and You are ever present to save and deliver me through them all. Amen.

Cultivating Our Then-Cry to the Lord

Then they cried to the LORD in their trouble,
and he delivered them from their distress.
Psalm 107:6 ESV

Have you discovered a distressful season in your life
when your spiritual footing was challenged? Perhaps you,
like me, have entertained misbeliefs and tried doing things
in your own strength or preferred timing. But our secure
footing wasn't secure after all because it wasn't based on
God's best—His truth.

The prodigal son in Luke 15 discovered this to be true
in his life. The younger of two sons, he decided he knew
better than his father and demanded his inheritance in
advance—before his father's death. In his distress and
frustration, he *told* his father, rather than *petitioning* him.

The prodigal's father granted his son's arrogant bid,
watched him pack his personal belongings and venture off
days later to destinations unknown.

Ultimately the boy squandered his entire gift on
wasteful and corrupt spending. Finding himself in a half-
starved condition, he resorted to work feeding pigs—a
humiliating position since pigs were considered an unclean
defilement. Under Moses' law, the young man wasn't sup-

posed to eat pigs or even touch them. But in his poverty, he craved the food that they ate.

In his selfishness, the rebellious boy had chosen to stray from his home and the father who unconditionally loved him. Luke 15 concludes the story with a triumphant moment as the prodigal returned home in humility, willing to confess his sin and acknowledge his folly. Here he experienced his *then*-cry and was showered with his father's abundant mercy, fanfare, and joy as he was reinstated back into his family.

Psalm 107 examines four different types of distressed people: those who stray, some who rebel, those in anguish, and others who are lost. Let's review the different prodigal types and see how Scripture points us back home:

The Strayer—Psalm 107:4-7

Those who stray have drifted away from God. Separated, they wander without a defined destination and no place to call home. Hungry and thirsty, their souls collapse within themselves as if without spirit.

But *then* they cry out to the Lord, and He faithfully liberates them from their distress. He leads them to the right way—to a safe place their hearts can call home. Their fainted souls, now satisfied, stand up with the promise of God's deliverance.

The Rebel—Psalm 107:10-14

Those who revolt against the words and ways of God experience a bleak existence of wrongdoing. Darkness as opposed to light. God's counsel is spurned, and life is reduced to the presence of death's shadow.

But *then* they reach out to God with humble hearts and He rescues them—shows the way out of their anarchy by breaking the bands that bind them in their rebellion. They are imprisoned no longer.

The Anguished—Psalm 107:17-20

Those who agonize because of foolish decisions suffer afflictions in soul and body. Their heartache can result in emotional heartbreak, torment, and woe. With no appetite, they loathe their food. It's not until they cultivate their *then*-cry to the Lord that they encounter redemption. God saves and heals them from ravaging ruin, bringing deliverance.

The Directionless—Psalm 107:23-30

When people are without focus and direction, they're confused and void of destination. Shipwrecked and drowning in their storm, their souls dissolve and lose all strength due to their distress. Courage is lost and they brood, *I don't know what to do or where to go.* They wobble in their disoriented states without purpose until their *then*-cry to God. He calms their inner storm and stills them as He guides them back to His heart's desired shelter.

To the wanderers, the prisoners, the anguished, and the misplaced, Psalm 107:1-2 ESV exhorts: *"Oh give thanks to the LORD, for he is good, for his steadfast love endures forever! Let the redeemed of the LORD say so, whom he has redeemed from trouble."* This passage affirms God's resolute love, measureless kindness, and willingness to forgive and justify. Even when intimidating influences of life lead to wanderings and pressures from within and without, Christians can look to God who provides purpose, guidance, and rest, knowing He will deliver. With thanksgiving, therefore, humility and faith mix to rescue us.

Consider:
If you find yourself in any of these situations, be assured there's a loving Father who waits for His children.

Further Reading:
Moses' law – Leviticus & Deuteronomy
Israelites cry for help; God uses Gideon to deliver – Judges 6-8
Reward for humility – Proverbs 22:4
When one comes to his/her senses – Luke 15:17
Walk worthy of our calling with humility – Ephesians 4:1-3
If we stray – Psalm 107:4-7
If we rebel – Psalm 107:10-14
If we're anguished – Psalm 107:17-20
If we're directionless – Psalm 107:23-30

Prayer:
Father, as I humble myself with a yielded heart, You rescue me. Thank You for making a redemptive way for me in every situation. With my mouth, I'll testify of Your unwavering love and faithful deliverance. Amen.

Cultivating Determination in Desperation

And behold, a woman who had suffered from a discharge of blood
for twelve years came up behind him and touched the fringe
of his garment, for she said to herself,
"If I only touch his garment, I will be made well."
Matthew 9:20-21 ESV

When we have finally had enough of a certain something in our life, we find ourselves in a desperate place. Do not despise this place but allow desperation to work for you.

When I was about 29 years old, I began to experience headaches. They interfered with my quality of life, especially since I was married, had a toddler about 1½ years old, and was returning to college after taking time off to be with our little boy. The headaches became more frequent and severe with the passage of time, and I made certain to carry acetaminophen with me when I left home.

Around the same time, I was learning about God's healing-promises outlined in Scripture. Identifying somewhat with the woman in the verse above, I felt desperate to touch the hem of Jesus' garment. I was determined, in my desperation, to discover action steps to eliminate these invaders. In addition to praying and requesting others to pray for me, I avoided certain foods that might trigger headaches. Three convictions stirred me in my quest for answers:

1. I felt impressed to acquire a boatload of books by Kenneth Hagin on the topic of healing and purposed to read them all.
2. I followed Scriptural protocol to pray for others' needs.
3. I determined to bless and praise God for His goodness—not for the headaches, but because of His innate goodness and loving kindness.

The deliverance manifested when I received prayer at a women's weekend retreat. I suffered with a nasty headache and nausea that evening. About 1:00 a.m. on that Sunday morning, I was the last woman to receive prayer and ultimately needed to leave the venue. Two friends from the meeting graciously drove me home. As I staggered into my house I collapsed in bed and slept.

It was about 3:00 p.m. the next afternoon when the headache dissipated. After that time, I no longer tangled with those wicked occurrences. Healed and delivered—all glory to God. My desperation followed by determination resulted in my deliverance.

I experience three positive outcomes when I allow desperation to do its work:

1. It compels me to my knees—In this humbled state, God has my undivided attention. I consecrate myself to Him with fresh awareness.
2. It purifies my desires and drives—Like fire purifies gold, the heat is on, and my spiritual senses heighten. I pay close attention to the Word of God, while most

of my typical chores and commitments get shuffled to the sidelines in place of the primary need.

3. It helps me to stay focused as to my God-ordained purposes in the earth—I recognize, meditate on, and sort out what is really important. Prayerfully, I examine my current life-situation to discern if I need to make any fundamental adjustments. *Am I on course with my God-intended purposes?*

When I reach bottom, I wonder, *How desperate am I for the healing-answer to my prayer?* I consider if I really want to be well. And I also honestly ask myself if I'm willing to make the necessary changes to live better.

We do not need to walk this road alone. During trials, we maintain determination and find comfort as we hope in God. While on our knees, we're in God's throne room where we humbly, yet boldly, approach Him by faith. If we decide to make changes and seek Him wholeheartedly, we have the opportunity to connect with Him.

Scriptures of promise provide us with hope and comfort while we walk this journey out. Acts 17 reveals God's desire for all to seek Him—finding their way toward Him as He is not distant. He's rescued me numerous times for which I am forever grateful.

Consider:
How have you experienced breakthrough with trials when you earnestly sought the Lord? Recount what you did to overcome in these situations.

Further Reading:
Scriptures of promise—Deuteronomy 4:29, Jeremiah 29:13
Do I really want to be well—John 5:5-7

Trials of life—James 1:2-4

Prayer:

Father, while pursuing You, my Healer, I reach out by faith. I resolve to be steadfast—to rise above obstacles for the fulfillment of Your answers. Thank You. Amen.

Cultivating Fearlessness

He is not afraid of bad news; his heart is firm,
trusting in the Lord.
Psalm 112:7 ESV

When fear tries to nudge itself into first place in your heart, what do you do?

Fear is a bully. When fear comes to plant an altar in my heart, I'm learning—notice learning—to slay it when it strikes. God is not the author or the deliverer of fear and torment, but rather it is Satan—the evil one. Fear manifests in numerous ways to paralyze, unnerve, and dominate.

One key way to counter fear is to trust in the Lord. When God seems to place me in situations where I am forced, per se, to trust Him.

One significant occasion occurred several years ago when our son was in the military ready to deploy to Afghanistan for a year. My husband, daughter, and I took him to the airport early on a Sunday morning. We stood in the terminal hugging once, twice, and again, then waved goodbye and blew kisses with our eyes fastened upon him until he was gone . . . gone beyond our visual sight and physical touch.

In the news, we heard about other servicemen and women deploying, but this time was different. This was our son, our daughter's brother. It suddenly was tangible, real, and fierce.

As my husband drove us home, a deafening silence engulfed us. I recall trying to pull myself up and out of a fearful, grief-like sensation that seemed to smother me. When we arrived home, I went up to my bed, tears clouding my eyes with a sorrowful presence. I was afraid to allow myself to feel this hopeless emotion.

I lazed restlessly, and after two hours, the still-small voice nudged me to *Get up, go downstairs, and make a cup of tea.* I knew this was God's prompt, and I also knew that if I didn't do it, I would slink down into a dark, depressive-like pit of helplessness and hopelessness.

I prepared the tea and muddled through some mundane tasks. When afternoon arrived, I decided to go to the mall to return an item. Not long after my arrival there, I met a friend I hadn't seen in a while, and we began to chat. I told her of our son's departure that morning and she revealed that her son had just returned from a deployment to Afghanistan.

She told me of her experience–her mother-heart–while he was away and now that he had returned. As she testified of God's faithfulness and goodness, the Lord quickened to my heart loud and clear that I had a choice—it stared me straight in the face: *I could worry about our son for the next 365 days* or *I could trust God to protect and keep him for the next year.*

A captivating sense of calmness settled upon me with a newfound capability to trust God with our son's life. That meeting at the mall was a divine connection—a God-orchestrated encounter. In a moment I was delivered from fear—an idolatrous dominator—by obeying God's voice and leading as I put my trust in Him.

God wants us to listen for His still small voice, do what He says, and trust Him implicitly. *Get up, Chris, and make the tea. Return the item to the mall store now. Receive my deliverance from this oppressive fear that attempts to bully you by stealing your peace and more for the next 365 days.*

Be encouraged as you place your trust in God. He will ransom you.

Consider:
Is there a tyrannical fear tormenting you? If so, what's the next step God is whispering for you to do? Please go forward in confident action and trust receiving God's best: deliverance from captivating idolatrous fear!

Further Reading:
Anxious thoughts and forebodings—Proverbs 15:15
Be not troubled, but pray—Philippians 4:6
God does not send or use fear against us—2 Timothy 1:7
The steps of a good man—Psalm 37:23
Meditate on and memorize—Isaiah 41:10
When I am afraid—Psalm 56:3

Prayer:
Father, when fear is tempting to overpower me, I place my trust in You. Thank You for making a way of escape when the alarm of fear strikes. Amen.

Author's Note:
I understand from Scripture that unfounded, paralyzing fear is an evil spirit sent by Satan to inflict harm and suffering. God has given us authority over Satanic attacks including

this kind of fear (Luke 10:19). For the purpose in the above story, I described how God delivered me from this crippling fear that tried to steal my peace. The emphasis on obedience and trust in Him were paramount. These were the ways He rescued me through a tormenting situation. All glory to God.

Cultivating a Heart that Seeks and Finds

"Then you will call upon me and come and pray to me, and I will hear you. You will seek me and find me, when you seek me with all your heart. I will be found by you, declares the LORD."
Jeremiah 29:12-14a ESV

Does it matter *what* we eat? I invest the time at the grocery store to search for the healthy stuff because it's important to me. I read labels to better avoid processed foods with hydrogenated fats, autolyzed yeast, carrageenan, and artificial colors. It may be a chore, but I'm willing to do it in order to find foods that will be nutrient dense and fuel my family and me with healthy choices.

As I'm willing to invest time, energy, and money in nourishing foods, I similarly choose to fuel my spirit. I devote time and awareness to seek and find the ways God wants to feed, strengthen, correct, and sustain me. It's important to search and discover that which genuinely serves my body, soul, and spirit—the healthiest choices in life.

Cultivating a hunger after God and desire for His ways, anticipates His blessings and opens our hearts to His direction. As our bodies cannot live long without food or water, our spirits weaken, even to the point of deterioration, without proper attention

Have you ever seen a ravenous bear? I've not seen one up close and personal, but I have seen video clips of hungry bears craving food around woodland cabins and campsites. They scrounge about and eat from unsecured trash bins. They claw, growl, and may even break windows, determined to eat at any cost. Hunger is a desperate need.

Do we crave hearing from God with such a desperate, seeking heart?

Cultivating a heart that seeks after the things of the Lord with such passion is learned with practice. As we park ourselves quietly with our focus on God, we often feel His peace settling our hearts and minds, like a tempered breeze on a balmy summer evening. All distractions resisted—the chirping phone, the growling stomach, the soiled laundry—it is possible to tune into Him like you'd tune to your favorite radio station.

God is neither magical nor mystical; we need not be apprehensive when prayerful before Him. He is our Creator. He's a Spirit. He seeks to communicate with our spirits. We can know Him by His still small voice speaking to our hearts usually in quiet promptings: "My sheep hear my voice, and I know them, and they follow me," John 10:27 ESV.

As I expect to find Him, I also recognize His guidance in church, the Scriptures, Christian programs, and insightful books and music. These provide answers to my hungering heart. They refresh my questioning and thirsty spirit like cool sparkling water on a hot summer's day. My heart is joy-filled as He faithfully satisfies. This is abundant life.

Only Jesus can fulfill our hearts and souls. Don't be duped into thinking material things can satisfy—it's Jesus who sustains. Seek Him with all your heart and expect Him to meet you in your place of longing and need.

Consider:

If you've felt starved spiritually, in what ways do you receive inspiration from God? When He prompts you, what action do you apply?

Further Reading:

Get to know God—1 Chronicles 28:9
Honor God with stillness—Psalm 46:10
Respond to God's beckoning—Psalm 27:8

Prayer:

Father, thank You for being true to Your promise in meeting us when we wholeheartedly search for and expect You. Amen.

114

LIGHT

His Light in our life
warms and nurtures
our family and social lives.

Cultivating a Parental Heart

For he satisfies the longing soul, and the hungry soul
he fills with good things.
Psalm 107:9 ESV

While growing up, when I was in middle school, I wondered why I felt an emptiness deep within—like there was a missing puzzle piece in my heart and soul. My parents loved me and would have done anything for me. But even though I loved my family and they loved me, I realized they couldn't give me what they did not have.

When I grew into a young twenty-something, I was introduced to the Living Savior—that missing puzzle "peace." Jesus Christ desired a personal relationship with me! My mind opened, my heart softened, and my spiritual blindness lifted as I accepted His offer of saving grace. Since that time, I have not looked back.

As parents, we cannot fill the empty places in our children's lives. We are not their missing puzzle piece. We want to be, but we can't be. Only the Spirit of God can fill and complete them since they are made in His image and belong to Him. As St. Augustine of Hippo stated in his famous *Confessions*, "You have made us for yourself, O Lord, and our heart is restless until it rests in you."

After a few years of marriage, my husband and I desired to start our family and asked God for children. He gifted us with two—our greatest treasures. We did our best to raise them, through our imperfections, and relied on wisdom from our wondrous God. He taught us to train them in godly ways and do everything we knew to do under the Lord's direction to cultivate within them the longing soul Psalm 107:9 speaks of. Even so, we watched them grow imperfectly.

Imperfectly because we cannot be God to them and fill the void in their hearts that wants and needs to be infused by their divine Maker. They, as we, are designed with a deep need for the Lord every day until their last breath.

As parents we know we are not our children's Savior, but rather a buttress of prayer, wisdom, counsel, refuge, and friendship. Although we love our friends, our favorite people are those two individuals who, as grown children, have become our best friends. We've enjoyed them and the relationship we've shared as they've grown into godly adults.

To cultivate a godly parental heart, give your children to Jesus so they can work out their own salvation with fear and trembling, consecrating themselves to God. Give them Jesus so they will know Who to run to when they're afraid, when they must make both peripheral and paramount decisions, and when they are hurt or disheartened. Steward them well and enjoy every season of life together!

Consider:
In what ways have you wanted to be everything to your children? How can you discover freedom as a parent if, and when, you released them into God's loving care?

Further Reading:
God satisfies the longing soul—Psalm 107:9
Consecrating themselves to God—Philippians 2:12

Prayer:
Father, since You're the only One who can gratify our souls, if I am holding too tightly to my children, please help me entrust them to You. You are the Father who knows best. Amen.

Cultivating the Bent in Our Children

Train up a child in the way he should go [teaching him to seek
God's wisdom and will for his abilities and talents],
Even when he is old, he will not depart from it.
Proverbs 22:6 AMP

Some years ago, Christian psychologist and author, Dr. James Dobson recommended that parents allow their children to try numerous different activities to discover what they enjoyed, identify their talents, and pursue their gifts earnestly. These pursuits might be sports-related, music and/or art-centered, or scholastically tilted.

My husband and I did this to a degree, given the time and resources we had. Our son played soccer and took drum lessons for a short time. He especially enjoyed camping and trail-hiking in Royal Rangers with some responsible men in our church. He participated in numerous camping trips that were challenging and invigorating, while he learned survival techniques.

Our daughter took piano and art lessons. Her creative talents surfaced and shimmered as she enjoyed different forms of art and music. Many years of practice at the piano resulted in her ability to feel at ease and at home with music theory and numerous music genres. She was an avid reader and later discovered that the field of health and wellness intrigued her.

As the children grew older, they participated in several different sports at school including basketball, volleyball, and track. They both participated in dramatic plays in their school with the skill to transform into their character's image.

Pay close attention to your children's desires, strengths, and sensitivities and notice how they respond to people and situations. Do they cry when someone else hurts or instead do they try to resolve the situation with an action that might attempt to fix the problem? Do they have leadership tendencies, advising others what to do, or are they faithful followers who come alongside to assist a leader with principled support?

The opening Scripture holds a key as we discern the particular bent in our children. According to author and speaker, Cynthia Tobias, she discovered the word "train" in this particular verse literally translates "to create an environment for life." This environment is one in which the child is self-assured, finds enjoyment, and thrives.

As Tobias suggests, parents ought to closely observe their children in order to discover their strengths and then focus on them. What do the children do well? Where and when are they cheerful and content? Depending upon what is learned, provide opportunities for them via activities conducive to their personalities and learning styles.

As we read our children in these ways, we recognize their unique God-appointed bents and assist with cultivating them. We shepherd them to seek God's will and wisdom that align with their abilities and skills.

In his teen years, our son provided spiritual and moral support to other members on his track team and befriended schoolmates who were shy. He exercised this gift for relating to people when, as a young adult, he engaged in street-ministry to strangers and lonely souls. This later led him to military service as a chaplain.

Our daughter excelled in playing numerous musical instruments and is an exceptional musician and instructor today. She is skilled and suited to connect both with her students' different personalities and their abilities. In addition to her role as a music instructor, our daughter connects with clients as a fitness specialist and a nutritional consultant—meeting their holistic needs in body, mind, and spirit.

Dedicate yourself to cultivating God's bent in each child you minister to—as parent, grandparent, or in some teaching capacity. Observe and listen to them closely to see their unique leaning surface. Study them, like a textbook, as if you are reading their hearts through God's eyes.

Consider:

As you commit to intentionally notice and train your children according to their individual bents, how will you accomplish this important mission?

Prayer:

Father, may we be sensitive to You and to the design You've placed in our children by listening well and training them according to their individual bent. We place our trust in You as we steward Your precious sons and daughters. Amen.

Cultivating Grace in the Empty Nest Season

Give ear, O Lord, to my prayer; listen to my plea for grace.
Psalm 86:6 ESV

Did your empty-nest chapter in life arrive too suddenly for you?

My role as a mom surpassed in importance various employment ventures, educational and ministry opportunities. It was the most valued mission in my life.

When the empty-nest season materialized, I experienced a personal loss. I loved being with my children—being home in the summer with them, including them on trips to the grocery store and on other errands, and I took great joy in recurrent library outings. I'm sure I enjoyed these times more than they did. Nevertheless, the brief season we shared was a dream for me.

The loss I felt in my empty nest was unexpected because I thought I'd sufficiently prepared for it. When it struck, it felt like a punch to the gut. I thought about my own parents, who modeled the empty nest season by graciously releasing my siblings and me as we each left in our turn. Why couldn't I do that? What was my problem? *Surely, I know better than to feel such a loss. I knew to expect this normal and natural time in life. Why do I feel like I just got knocked to the floor without a cushion to soften the fall?*

Our son left first to a college out-of-state and eventually entered military service. Our daughter left a few years later to room with a girlfriend. We enjoyed our visits with each other, but it was different from their living in our home.

In my struggle, my son encouraged me to put things in perspective—seeing the situation from his vantage point. Our home was no longer his home. Where he currently resided was his home. Could I accept that?

Shortly after our daughter moved out, she invited me to spend the night at her place on her very comfy spare bed at the end of a rigorous college semester. A decade later, I can still feel the blessing of her offer to spend the night, the crisp sheets on the bed, and waking up to a rustic view outside the window. There were birds, wildlife, and quietude—even peacocks from the neighborhood that perched on her rooftop. How could I not take joy in seeing her so well situated. I savored my mini-vacay time with her as we munched on meals and shopped later that day.

While our son was in college, he often invited us to visit him. He would gift us with a stay in a nearby hotel. We shared daytime hours together and enjoyed him as a gracious host. We loved our family reunions!

It helps our children to see me happy for them as they live life on their own. I had to learn that when I expressed too much disappointment as a phone call or a visit ended, it was hard on them. To appreciate all the moments we share when together is a treasure and should be prioritized and cherished with a grateful heart—not dismay that the moment came to an end.

I'm happy to report after many bumpy encounters, tears, and mistakes, I've landed on the other side of empty-nest angst enjoying this new season in my life. My husband, a quiet strength through it all, reassures me with words of encouragement should I weaken.

Here are some helpful actions I've learned and adopted through counseling studies and on my own when adjusting to empty-nest living:

- Be happy for your children upon their departure — it's not all about you.
- Resist wallowing in self-pity when you have to end a visit together or a phone conversation. You might not realize you're doing this, but if you are, like I once did — stop! It's not supportive or earnest.
- Delight in the moments you share together — seize them as cherished encounters.
- Invite your children to your home for a meal or a visit, but if they cannot accept, let it go rather than act disappointed. Everyone has different schedules and sometimes the demands of their work or family delay dinner dates.
- Prepare for empty nest reality with a commitment to look forward to your new stage in life before they leave home. Prepare a vision and a plan for the post-childrearing years.
- Re-frame your thoughts to be thankful and satisfied in a job well done that you have raised independent and responsible children able to step out into the world.
- Re-frame your thoughts to view this time as a treasured season to re-acquaint yourself with your spouse.
- Re-frame your thoughts to reach out intentionally and build or re-build relationships with girlfriends.

- Re-frame your thoughts to enjoy the flexibility of mealtimes, date nights, and undertaking projects that were postponed while you were raising your children. Perhaps, like writing a book.
- Re-frame your thoughts to relish more quality time with your Savior through increased Bible study and prayer.

Empty-nest season is a time of transition on many fronts. It can hit hard because there are other changes occurring at the same time in a woman's life such as menopause, changes in physical appearance, our role as nurturing-mother evolving into that of confidante and friend, and the reality of parents aging and passing away.

For a smooth transition, educate yourself with fact-based reading and research materials to help you understand and cruise through this season of life. Connect with mature women in the faith who have already completed this chapter of life successfully.

Then, do yourself a favor and seize each day beginning with prayer! Ask God to include you in and alert you to His plans for that day. Watch how some ordinary days revolutionize to extraordinary ones. Seek His empowerment to live content in this new empty-nest season in His generous grace.

Consider:

How have you actively prepared for the empty-nest season in your life? If you identified with any of the struggles I expressed, what supportive actions did you apply to transition through this new adventure?

Further Reading:
For from his fullness, we have all received, grace upon grace—John 1:16
Children are an inheritance from the Lord—Psalm 127:3
The children of the righteous are blessed—Psalm 112:1-2

Prayer:
Father, thank You for the privilege of motherhood. May we, as wives and mothers, receive your gift of grace to navigate our different seasons employing Your direction and wisdom. Escorted by Your grace, may we learn how to prepare for these natural changes. Amen.

Cultivating the Gift of Slack

And as you wish that others would do to you, do so to them.
Luke 6:31 ESV

After my husband and I finished our "discussion," I asked him what he wanted from me. His reply: "I just want you to give me some slack."

Ouch! But yes. He was right. And I wanted to do better.

Slack is probably way underrated. In moments of disagreement, we usually side with ourselves because we know our motives. *I didn't mean anything wrong. I had no ill intentions.* Giving the other party slack doesn't enter the room because we believe *we* need slack from them.

Extending slack is no small thing. When I render forbearance to others, I reproduce the character of Christ. The Scripture teaches God's tolerance with humanity as He withholds wrath, patiently waiting while He forgives our many offenses. With patience, God tarries, waiting for His children to modify their minds and actions to His way of thinking and doing life. God's forbearing kindness is intended to steer us toward contriteness of heart.

In my counseling studies, I've learned people often act more inconsiderately and critically toward those they live with and love the most. When people lean in this direction, they often grant greater respect and tolerance to friends, colleagues, and those they hardly know. Ironically, a double standard surfaces.

Biblical wisdom prescribes tolerance and a forgiving spirit as we interact with others—in essence, slack. Especially to those closest to us. There will be times when we require forgiveness and forbearance from others. Therefore, release others with a generous granting of slack to cultivate win-win conditions.

For those of us who are married, let's intentionally give our spouses honor and respect, which God considers holy behavior. There are no perfect marriages, but we can make our marriages better when we start with ourselves and apply loving action to our words. If we find ourselves engaging in "lively discussion," let's remember to discuss and play fairly, allowing plenty of slack.

Consider:

What are some ways you've provided slack to others or perhaps failed to do so? Think specifically about how you can strengthen your close relationships by granting slack to them and commit to your resolve to do so by recording your thoughts in a journal.

Further Reading:

Holy behavior—Ephesians 5:22-33
Forgiving spirit—Matthew 6:14-15; Ephesians 4:32
Forbearance—Romans 2:4

Prayer:

Father, may my heart be humble and contrite in Your sight. It's my desire to walk closer with You by offering good will, slack, and forbearance to others. Amen.

Cultivating Our Go and Tell:
In Season and Out

"I charge you in the presence of God and of Christ Jesus, who is to judge the living and the dead, and by His appearing and His kingdom: preach the word; be ready in season and out of season; reprove, rebuke, and exhort, with complete patience and teaching. For the time is coming when people will not endure sound teaching, but having itching ears they will accumulate for themselves teachers to suit their own passions."
2 Timothy 4:1-3 ESV

My husband and I were preparing to fly home to New Jersey from a visit with our son and daughter-in-law. I took one final walk on the dazzling emerald coastline. I feasted on our final moments there as a slight breeze caressed my face. I welcomed the sunshine as it warmed my body and heart. I listened to the rhythmic pulse of the sparkling green waves as they beat against the shoreline.

Before I'd left our hotel room, I'd stashed a few Gospel tracts with bite-sized messages explaining the love of God in my belt bag. Part of my morning mission was to offer them to fellow beach-walkers. I whispered a brief prayer: *Father, please lead me to those with whom I can share Your message of love.*

I took advantage of three separate opportunities to approach people during my final 45 minute-beach walk. As I offered a tract I said, "Good morning! Are you interested in receiving a pamphlet to learn more about Jesus?

Pause.

"When I came to know Jesus in a personal way, it made an amazing change in my life and I've never regretted it."

Smile.

Not pushy. Non-threatening. Not overbearing. No ulterior motive. Just wanting to offer the Gospel—an opportunity for eternal life—to a person passing by.

Two people responded, "No, thanks, I'm okay," and the other said he already knew the Lord.

As I returned to the hotel room I understood my part was to go and tell people about new life with Christ, to make an offer to them, but that each one has a free will to choose. While it's God's desire that all come to know and accept Him, it's never forced.

Shortly afterward, my husband and I headed for the airport to begin our trip home. It was a longer journey than we'd expected, with unexpected delays. Twelve hours later, I sandwiched in between two strangers on the final flight. Neither of them seemed bent toward engaging in conversation and I didn't want to connect either, feeling fatigued and done with the day.

Or so I thought.

About 40 minutes later, I felt an inner nudge to break the silence and compliment the woman to my left about the elaborate garment she was knitting. Once I spoke to her, she replied freely without reservation. She explained how knitting the sweater was a challenge, but she was determined to complete it. My opening comments led to a full-scale conversation about families, occupations, hobbies, and then . . . Jesus.

I sensed the Lord in the encounter—in a divine nudge. With a go-and-tell moment, I briefly shared the story when I submitted to Jesus, including how He was the answer to my vacuous heart.

Intrigued, she admitted she and her family were not at all religious, listened, and seemed sincerely interested. We departed the plane with cordial good-byes.

It was no accident we were seated next to each other on that flight. God had a plan, and I almost missed it in my weariness after a long travel day. It was crucial that I be ready out of season—when I didn't feel like engaging with someone—in order to share my faith with an earnest and inquisitive stranger. She was a lovely person who didn't make a commitment for Christ that night but left with something of paramount importance to contemplate.

There was eternity-value in both of the opportunities to go-and-tell on that day: my in-season, wide-awake morning shore walk and out-of-season final moments on a plane when almost home. The Word of the Lord never returns void—whether it's Scriptures in a tract or an unexpected encounter to share a real-life faith experience, boasting about a Real Savior.

Consider:

How have you responded to opportunities to share your faith when the timing was less than favorable for you? Think of some experiences when you've shared Jesus. Recount the thrill of these special moments and their eternity-value.

Further Reading:
The Great Commission—Mark 16:15
Set your minds on things above—Colossians 3:1-3

Prayer:
Father, Your last words to us were to fulfill the Great Commission—to go and tell people in our spheres of influence about Your greatness and the reality of becoming born again. May I be faithful to make what's important to You be important to me in season and out. I'm thankful for the freedom to share You with others and for the divine appointments You create to convey Your message of love. Amen.

Cultivating a Biblical Work Ethic

Whatever you do, work heartily, as for the Lord and not for men,
Colossians 3:23 ESV

In the familiar Aesop's Fable, *The Ant and the Grasshopper*, the grasshopper lived haphazardly—only for the moment and with no thought of the future.

One summer day, the grasshopper tried to coax the industrious ant to frolic about with him. "Come on. Let's have some fun. Leave that work for another day."

But the ant remained focused on his tasks. "Winter will be upon us before we know it! I must work to store up the food and goods I will need on harsh days."

The heedless grasshopper resisted the ant's wise words on the benefit and necessity of good work and chose to continue in his amusements. Soon the winter winds blew, and work could not be done. The ant settled cozy in his home with all he needed, ready and at hand, in the dark, cold days.

But the careless grasshopper regretted his foolish decision to spend all his summer season in play. He struggled, starved, and desperate for food and necessities begged the ant for a portion of his supplies. But the ant had no goods he could spare.

This simple tale offers profound wisdom for judicious living: Don't slumber today and expect surplus tomorrow.

Did the grasshopper regret his choice? What did he believe about life that led him to make bad decisions? Did he see his fault—or did he try to place the blame for his lack elsewhere?

Like the grasshopper, when people believe an untruth, they can make poor decisions. Even worse, they may believe God led them in their bad choices and blame Him when the results are less than desirable.

Referencing the female worker ant, Proverbs 6 illustrates the wisdom she applies as she works hard during summer to harvest in later months for the winter season. She does this with no taskmaster lording it over her because of her innate understanding of industriousness. It's simply part of who she is created to be.

The industry of work is God's plan. He modeled the balance of labor and rest in His own work pattern observed in the Creation account, as Genesis 2:2 NLT records, "On the seventh day, God had finished his work of creation, so he rested from all his work."

Don't be a grasshopper. Real Life Moms know the value of industry in life exercised joyfully within a balanced work ethic.

Consider:

Have you been tempted to assume money or means were going to chase you down separate from your investment? Explain. On the other hand, if you've nurtured a balanced work ethic, describe how you live it and the rewards you've realized through it.

Further Reading:
Honor bestowed upon skillfulness—Proverbs 22:29
A lesson from the ant—Proverbs 6:6-8

Prayer:
Father, may I work wholeheartedly in recognition of the opportunities You provide for me to responsibly steward my time in a balance of industry and rest. With all I do, may I complete the small and great tasks You've called me to as doing them unto You, rather than unto men. Amen.

Cultivating Church Life

And let us consider how to stir up one another to love and good
works, not neglecting to meet together, as is the habit of some,
but encouraging one another, and all the more
as you see the Day drawing near.
Hebrews 10:24-25 ESV

To church or not to church? This could be your question.

Numbers of churches are closing. Many people no longer corporately congregate while others watch or listen to services on the internet. This may be convenient for the home-bound, though many choose not to participate in church fellowships for diverse reasons.

Several years ago, when I was in a spiritually dry place, I pondered, *Is church over-rated?* On a given Sunday I appraised my personal church experience and noted some uplifting findings:

- During worship as the service began, the Holy Spirit edified my spirit as I honored Him with praise.
- My late pastor presented an inspiring sermon fortifying us to recognize God's Hand in our lives.
- The Holy Spirit lovingly corrected me using the pastor's words. I repented and tweaked my attitude.

136

- We prayed corporately for our government and for others' needs.
- I attended an invigorating Sunday school class involving a lively book discussion.
- Following the sermon my pastor asked me to join him to pray with several young students.
- Two friends and I briefly talked with and prayed for a friend who was troubled with a serious physical condition. He was greatly reassured.
- My husband and I offered an employment-lead to a friend.
- After reading the bulletin, I was reminded of a friend's upcoming birthday. The following week, I sent a card to remember her.

After my simple appraisal of church that Sunday morning, my spiritual eyesight sharpened. We may approach church with the mindset, *What can I get from attending church?* While this isn't a bad question to ask, we can better enter our sanctuary offering ourselves saying, *Father, how can I give of myself today? What do You want me to hear from You and others?* We go to church to be spiritually fed, but we also gather with believers to share what God has personally ministered to us throughout the prior week.

Each person is unique—no one else represents God like we do in our congregational settings. Each of our lives matters, and we're special in the way we touch our spheres of influence. My husband and I share a prayer on most mornings before we enter our church service: *Father, help us not to miss You today. May we be in step with what You're up to and reflect You to others.*

Finally, observing our lead Scripture, it's essential for us to gather together for several integral reasons:

1. It's Scriptural, therefore God's will.
2. We give thought to and care for one another.
3. We encourage others to participate in charitable acts.
4. Christ's Second Coming—His return—is imminent. As believers, we continue to exhort one another in our faith as this day approaches.
5. Jesus loved the Church.

Church gatherings edify believers in Christ. Our church congregation becomes a family as we build connections and friendships—some lasting a lifetime. I expect God to be present. Matthew 18:20 relates where two or more gather in Jesus' Name, He's among them.

When I attend church, I always discover what I expect to find—an inspiring experience. Go be a blessing and watch how God brightens your heart and pours out His love and goodness on you.

Consider:

In what ways is God speaking to you using this message? God convicts and encourages with a loving tone. He never condemns—Satan uses condemnation. If you do attend church, how can you challenge yourself to make a difference in your church family-sphere?

Further Reading:

God's presence among us—Matthew 18:20
Christ's Second Coming foretold—Luke 17
Jesus died for His Church—Ephesians 5:25-27

Prayer:

Father, thank You for the freedom to attend church without restriction and for my church family. I'm edified when I meet with my Christian brethren to worship You and to be used by You to stir up love and kind deeds among us. Amen.

Cultivating an Appetizing Lifestyle

*I am the vine; you are the branches. Whoever abides in me
and I in him, he it is that bears much fruit,
for apart from me you can do nothing.*
John 15:5 ESV

I watched the birds flock to the birdfeeder in my yard. Blue jays, cardinals, and goldfinches, with their striking blue, scarlet, and bright yellow jackets, exhibited a rainbow of color. Their fluttering wings and noble crests thrust me into their world of beauty. Melodious musical arrangements from the cardinals rendered cheerful strains. Their zeal to flit around the feeder and devour a morning meal clutched my curiosity with delight.

We knew sunflower seeds attract jays, cardinals, and finches, so we offered plenty of them. Finches relish thistle seed, too. We keep their seed dry and fresh to ensure routine, return visits. We love that they come here to be fed and filled by the feeder.

I want to attract people, like sunflower and thistle seeds attract birds, who are famished in a hollow world. Assuredly though, it is Jesus in me that makes me God-flavored. God's presence is what makes me appetizing to the world. Because Jesus resides in me, I can be His hands and feet on earth to captivate wanting hearts with true satisfaction. I desire to offer Jesus to those who search for fulfillment because only He forever satisfies.

Cultivating an appetizing lifestyle requires me to put away former ways of living—doing whatever I feel or choose. Instead, I must permit the abiding presence of the Lord to guide my life choices and respect the Holy Spirit's way of living according to the fruit of the Spirit.

The fruit of the Spirit develops in a person as a process. This is called sanctification. It produces Jesus' love, joy, peace, patience, kindness, goodness, gentleness, faithfulness, and self-control in the heart. These characteristics are not generated by the person herself, but rather from her yielding to the indwelling Spirit of God to reflect Christ's characteristics. A person's appetite changes from sinful natural tendencies to godly desires and traits stemming from the nature of Christ, as the Holy Spirit transforms her from the inside out. His nature becomes her new nature.

To cultivate the presence of the Lord in one's life, she does so by reading, considering, and beholding the living Word of God—the Bible. She builds strength in her inner person as she unifies with Christ, choosing to live and walk in the Spirit. Because there are two conflicting impulses in humanity's heart, cultivating a lifestyle of strength in the Holy Spirit is essential to abide in Christ and to attract people to the Lord.

Yielding my will to His ways mirrors Him more accurately for a hungry world. For Jesus to live loudly in me, I must abide in Him for Him to abide in me. Apart from Him, I cannot be savory or inviting. My lifestyle, rooted in Christ, produces fruit.

Ask yourself: Is my life a savory morsel for those who are spiritually starved? Have I lingered at the Master's Birdfeeder long enough to make a difference in who I am? To eat my fill in His presence and become an appetizing representation of Him in the earth?

Just a glance at world headlines proves we live among a population of undernourished people in places of fruitless influence. May we seek to be fruitful influencers and life-changing nourishment to satisfy the unmet cravings of a world starved for more of Jesus. We accomplish this when we preserve our lives in the Vine and keep ourselves pure and clean in mind and heart. We are then positioned for Jesus to tap us and draw upon us, ready for His use and our fulfillment of purpose in Him.

Remember: Lean on the Holy Spirit to empower you in His strength and ability as His fruit develops in you.

Consider:
How do you regularly position yourself to abide in Him as God Food in the earth and attract undernourished seekers?

Further Reading:
Walking in humility—John 3:30
Becoming all things to all people—1 Corinthians 9:22
Living life in the Holy Spirit; Fruit of the Spirit—Galatians 5:16-26

Prayer:
Father, while we abide in You, may we each cultivate a palatable lifestyle able to satisfy hungering hearts. Allowing You to continually stir our hearts, may we be inclined to draw near to You as You continue to grow big in us. Amen.

Cultivating Pleasure in Service

Serve the Lord with gladness!
Psalm 100:2a ESV

Ever been to a Chick-fil-A restaurant? After customers receive their meals and reply with "thank you" as they leave, the servers religiously respond with a hearty, "It's my pleasure!"

What polite and gracious words to hear—all due to a chicken sandwich! Perhaps we can learn a lesson from Chick-fil-A employees' pleasant attitudes and actions as they seek to please even the most difficult customers.

Is it my humble pleasure to serve and live for Jesus?

Is it my pleasure to willingly say "yes" to the hard places in my life if Jesus is directing me in such areas?

Is it my pleasure to die daily to the flesh, the carnal nature, which contrarily kicks and squeals while the Lord's Spirit within me whispers, *There's a better way; do it My way; My yoke is easy and My burden is light*?

Can we say with resolve, *It's my pleasure, Lord, to*:

- Die daily; to offer myself to Christ in preparation for eternal life—1 Corinthians 15:30-32
- Take up my cross and follow You, as I commit my life to You—Luke 9:23
- Forgive myself and/or others—Matthew 6:14-15

- Hold onto hope since You are with me and I won't be shaken—Psalm 16:8-10
- Resist being offended because You gave Yourself on the cross, the greatest expression of love—John 13 & 14
- Praise You through storms of life, since You rescue me from them all—Psalm 34:17; Matthew 5:44-46
- Walk after the Holy Spirit's might and not after the flesh—Galatians 5:16
- Submit myself to You and resist the seductive devil, for he will then run—James 4:7
- Remain standing in the time of evil attacks—Ephesians 6:13
- Rejoice in You continually—Philippians 4:4
- Allow my tongue to be ruled by the law of kindness—Proverbs 31:26
- Prefer and honor others—Romans 12:10

Tuck into close fellowship with the Holy Spirit as you grow in grace. Allow Jesus to realign you if you struggle with unprofitable habits, attitudes, and behaviors. He wants to ally with you and me when we get sidetracked and tripped up. Let's re-consecrate ourselves as we join our hearts together in the accommodating pleasure of our life service to Him. He, in turn, is pleased with the humble, granting them salvation.

Consider:
Take the time, energy, and effort to meditate on and practice any or all of these points listed in the days and weeks to come. We can witness God's transforming reflection of Himself in each of our lives.

Further Reading:

God's goal for us to be conformed to Christ's likeness—Romans 8:29

Prayer:

Father, it's my pleasure to serve You in the little and the big, the mundane and the majestic affairs of life. As I humble myself before You, You graciously clothe me with salvation. Thank You for the opportunities to minister to You. Amen.

Cultivating Service as a Lifestyle

Let love be without hypocrisy. Abhor what is evil. Cling to what is good. Be kindly affectionate to one another with brotherly love, in honor giving preference to one another; not lagging in diligence, fervent in spirit, serving the Lord;
Romans 12:9-11 NKJV

To build deeper relationships with others, my husband and I enjoy serving people with dinner invitations.

The more I invite folks to my home, the easier it is to serve them in varied ways. As my husband and I share conversation and fellowship with friends or family, we learn their needs. The connections we build matter more than the perfection of the food or how immaculate the house looks after dust bunnies have been secured in the belly of the vacuum cleaner.

There is something consequential about sitting across from a person and breaking bread with them in an intimate setting. We discover new things about people whom we thought we already knew well and minimize distractions to better focus on our guests.

Another way I serve others is to mentor one-on-one with young women—especially moms. I provide a safe space to listen to their heart and share wisdom snippets in conversation and prayer agreement. Sometimes we visit

146

over the phone, sometimes we meet in person or perhaps on a walk.

Serving others with your time and attention to answer questions, address uncertainties, and share dreams or laments is an invaluable gift in service to others. I commit myself as a conduit of the Holy Spirit to hush forebodings and quench a yearning heart which gladdens us both.

Service from a pure heart is key. Always check your motives to be sure the Holy Spirit guides you into your unique service assignment and leads in all decision making. Living a lifestyle of serving God and others fulfills God's call in your life as a sweet aroma, the fragrance of Christ in the earth.

Consider:
Each person possesses individualized gifts from God as listed in Romans 12:6-8. After reading the list, what acts of service are you currently fulfilling? If you aren't yet involved in service, what can you begin to do? As you commit this to prayer, God will show you and empower you to effectively serve.

Further Study:
Service with a humble heart—Matthew 20:26b-28
Reasonable service to God; gifts/talents—Romans 12:1-8

Prayer:
Father, help me to worship You by humbly and happily serving others as a reflection of Your character and disposition. Help me, also, to be sensitive to Your leading as I endeavor to stay in step with Your plans. Amen.

Cultivating Balance in Service as a Lifestyle

Search for the Lord and for his strength; continually seek him.
Psalm 105:4 NLT

When serving God and others becomes a lifestyle, God is pleased, and others are edified. While service to others is a regular part of our lives, we must seek to live balanced, with a conscious effort to employ self-care. Though I'm usually cognizant to do so, there have been times when I've taken on commitments which resulted in burdens I wasn't meant to bear.

Some years ago, I was asked to fill a two to three month, after-school program coaching girls' volleyball at the Christian school where I worked. I quickly responded that I would serve and gave no thought to how it might impact my family. My children would have to wait after school four days a week, lengthening our already full day by two and a half hours. My husband, though a patient man, would be forced to come home to an empty house on those days, awaiting our return.

We all survived my impetuous decision, but I realized that it wasn't wise for me to answer that particular call to extra service. It adversely affected my gracious family members. I failed to inquire of the Lord as to whether my good intention to serve as coach was meant for me. I would have done well to follow King David's example in Scripture: make it part of my lifestyle of service to inquire of the Lord first. Ask for God's guidance before plunging ahead into battle—or service opportunities.

Allow the Holy Spirit of God to guide and lead in all your decision-making regarding acts of service to secure a balance of work, rest, and daily renewal—both spiritual and practical. Implement these self-care practices in order to serve well:

- Beware of over-commitments not ordained by God. Don't say "yes" to a service opportunity as an automatic reflex. Sometimes we need to say, *"I'm sorry; I cannot do it this time."*
- Seek the Lord's wisdom and guidance. He knows what lies ahead. Seek Him to discern if certain ministries of service are His will for you. Stay in your own lane. Speak and live authentically before the Lord.
- Consult with family members regarding an act of service that may involve or affect them.
- Consider if the timing of the service, ministry, or project is fitting when added to other existing obligations.
- Care for yourself through rest, diet, and exercise so you'll have the strength to give to others. Schedule time for personal rest and renewal into your days to avoid burn-out.
- Communicate your needs without complaining.
- Request help to build a team, if necessary.
- Slay self-pity, resentment, and pride, which creep in when we're tempted to think we are doing more than

others. *Oh, poor me . . . Look at all I've done.* Resist a critical spirit and cultivate a grateful attitude.

When we implement practical guardianship over our lifestyle habits, we ethically serve others and God. Locate the right balance between godly service and responsible self-care as you allow the Lord to lead you into every life assignment to His glory.

Consider:
What forms of self-care nurtures you so you can fruitfully serve others well? If you've overextended yourself with service projects in the past, what did you learn that can help you not overextend yourself again?

Further Reading:
Meditate on the following Scriptures with examples of how often David inquired of the Lord: 1 Samuel 23:2; 1 Sam. 23:4; 1 Sam. 30:8; 2 Sam. 2:1; 2 Sam. 5:19. How many more references can you find?

Prayer:
Father, help me to be honest with myself and You as I worship You with the tasks and ministries I cheerfully accept. I purpose to responsibly care for myself in body and spirit in order to effectively serve You and others. Amen.

Cultivating Service as Worship

*But the Lord answered her, "Martha, Martha, you are anxious
and troubled about many things, but one thing is necessary.
Mary has chosen the good portion,
which will not be taken away from her.*
Luke 10:41-42 ESV

What do you think of when you hear the word
worship? For some, the meaning of worship is the music we
sing at church or play in our home. True worship, though, is
much more than music and song.

Luke 10 recounts the visit Jesus made to His friends
Mary and Martha and their preparation to serve the Master.
They both served Him with their love and worship but in
different ways. Martha prepared, perhaps, an elaborate
meal for her special guest. The text infers she was quite busy
anticipating the event with much to do. Mary welcomed
Jesus with a more intimate worship. Rather than help
Martha with the material preparations, she sat at His feet to
hear Him teach and talk to her. As she gazed into His eyes
and heart, she gleaned from Him all she could while He was
present in her home.

Which sister exhibited the more meaningful worship?
Jesus addressed the situation telling Martha she was anxious
about much while Mary had chosen the better thing. Could

it be that He was preparing Mary with understanding that would be lifesaving and life-changing for her future? What she didn't know at the time was how her faith would be tested soon in the death of her brother Lazarus—and his subsequent resurrection. Could it be the things He shared with her would be truths she ultimately would need to lean into and present to others as ministry to them?

Only Jesus knew what Mary would do with what He told her. He made the point that Mary's expression of service prioritized her close relationship with Him. She chose to serve Him with her undivided attention, sitting at His feet over all the busy work that seemed wanting.

In his book *Morning and Evening*, nineteenth century English preacher and author, Charles Spurgeon, addressed the topic of service as inspired by this passage. He faulted Martha's anxious attitude when she grew "cumbered about much serving" as noted in Luke 10:40. Spurgeon compared Mary's worshipful response to Jesus' visit with that of her busy sister Martha. He explained that while serving is necessary, Martha forgot about Jesus Himself and "allowed service to override [her] communion" with Him.

While Martha's and Mary's roles in service were both necessary, Spurgeon's wisdom speaks to our hearts with impact: "The first thing for our soul's health, the first thing for his glory, and the first thing for our own usefulness, is to keep ourselves in perpetual communion with the Lord Jesus."

We profit best when we model Mary's behavior as she first sat, stilled, at Jesus' feet and yielded full attention to His teaching. It is important for us to remember that worthy worship unto God and service to others begins with having first lingered in the Lord's presence as He shares His heart with us.

Consider:
How have you been reserving time to sit at the Master's feet? How have you sensed His prompting you to *Come away with Me, my child*? What invaluable riches has Jesus whispered to your heart as you've communed with Him?

Further Reading:
Devoted communion—Psalm 27:8
Lazarus' death and resurrection—John 11

Prayer:
Father, as Mary did, may I exhibit a surrendered mind and heart and tarry in Your presence to discover what's important to You before I launch into my ministry of busy. Amen.

Cultivating Friendships

A man of many companions may come to ruin,
but there is a friend who sticks closer than a brother.
Proverbs 18:24 ESV

Isn't it a joy to have a faithful friend? A BFF—best friend forever?

Jesus can be that friend to us. The above Scripture affirms He is that One who will be closer than all others.

When I was a college student in 1983, I met a woman who would become a forever friend. Although we weren't best friends, it was a stable relationship built on loyalty, sincerity, and grace. She and I shared a few classes together, occasionally went to lunch, and enjoyed similar interests as we pursued the same major of study.

After graduation, she and her husband moved out of state, but we maintained friendship corresponding with cards and emails, often including prayer support. She was an artist, so on every birthday and at Christmas she sent a card with her personal artwork. For many years she also sent Christmas packages with gifts for each member of my family including our dog. In my home, I modestly framed most of the cards she painted, and they grace our walls each season. She passed to Heaven in 2020, but her memory will always remain in my heart as a faithful and true friend.

Based on Jesus' behavior with His disciples and those to whom He ministered, several defining characteristics manifest with true friendship:

- **Faithful**—Jesus maintained friendship with His disciples until His death—even when many of them abandoned Him at one time or another.
- **Forgiving**—Jesus was forgiving when Judas betrayed Him, when Peter denied Him, when His friends in the Garden of Gethsemane deserted Him, when the thief on the cross asked for forgiveness, and when the mob of humanity crucified Him.
- **Generous**—Jesus was generous with His attention, energy, and compassion when people approached Him with needs.
- **Service**—Jesus exhibited a servant-heart when washing the disciples' feet, feeding the hungry multitudes, and responding to parents' cries on behalf of sick and/or demon-possessed children.

After polling fifteen women of various ages, I compiled their definitions of true-hearted friendship. Hearing from them helps me to know how to actively demonstrate my care for others' interpretation of faithful friendship.

- **Acceptance**—She supports you, allows you to be yourself, doesn't try to change you, and loves you even at your worst.
- **Confidential**—She maintains privacy and is trustworthy.
- **Encourager**—She supports you with motivating words and actions and makes you feel valued and respected.

155

- **Listener**—She provides her undivided attention.
- **Faithful**—She's loyal and dedicated to you and to the Lord, active in her Christian walk, seeking to grow stronger.
- **Celebrates & Mourns**—She both rejoices and grieves with you.
- **Speaks Truthfully**—She speaks openly with honest conversation.
- **Accommodates**—She helps you feel at ease, relaxed, and safe in her presence and provides comfort by letting you be yourself.
- **Advice**—She offers compassionate counsel when warranted.
- **Knows You**—She takes the time and interest in who you are and what you do. She may be able to finish your sentences and even if you've been apart for a season, you can still feel connected.
- **Prays**—She intercedes for you—sometimes in secret.
- **Acknowledges Jesus**—She admits that Jesus is the most faithful and truest friend available and appreciates sharing the Lord with you as a friend.
- **Enjoyment**—She is someone with whom you can laugh and have fun.

Cultivating friendship includes the wisdom found in Proverbs 17:17 which observes that a friend loves at all times—not just when it's convenient. It's commendable when we make room for other people's interests, joys, griefs, and burdens.

In order to cultivate friendship, there must be some sacrifice involved. Jesus' divine rule was and remains for us to love each other like He selflessly loves us. He sacrificially laid down His life for us—the greatest expression of loving friendship.

If you desire to cultivate faithful friendship, reach out to others. Make the call. Send the note. Listen well. Be present when together. Consider them on purpose. Remember them in prayer. Thank God for their lives and the gift of their friendship!

Consider:
What can you do to be the kind of friend you desire your friends to be to you? What changes and actions are involved in your decisions?

Further Reading:
Jesus' commandment to love—John 15:12-13
The Golden Rule—Matthew 7:12; Luke 6:31

Prayer:
Father, help me to be the kind of friend I long for. May I be challenged to faithful action as I study and adopt Jesus' model of friendship towards others with a thankful heart. Amen.

Cultivating Comfort for Those Who Grieve

Blessed are those who mourn, for they shall be comforted.
Matthew 5:4 ESV

Everyone faces grief at some time in their lives. We grieve over losses due to the death of loved ones, friends, and beloved pets. We grieve over emotional losses, as well: fractured relationships, divorce, personal violations, employment termination, financial and material loss. The depth of the woundedness may vary; nevertheless, everyone experiences pain and grief in this life.

I experienced a personal loss upon my parents' deaths. My mother passed away first. From as early as I can remember, I loved my mother dearly. It was difficult when I married and moved from my home in upstate New York to my new residence in New Jersey, but I was determined to see my mother about three times a year.

After our children were born, our family continued to journey to New York and enjoyed visits with my parents, my sister, and her family. We shared phone calls and hand-written letters, too. My mom's passing punctured my heart. I felt the loss as a grievous sting.

Four years after my mother's death, my father passed away. Because he was my surviving parent, saying goodbye to him was more difficult. By this time, my siblings and I had to travel anywhere from 200 to over 2000 miles to visit him.

During those four years, and especially his final year, my dad and I grew closer than ever. Together, we'd chat as we strolled down the hallway of his apartment building—I spotted him while he commanded his walker. We enjoyed car rides as I chauffeured him around and exchanged warm conversations—not too deep stuff, but deeper than we'd shared in the past.

Dad had been diagnosed with late-stage stomach cancer. During some of the many hospitalizations he braved, we discussed his personal wishes regarding end-of-life decisions. My siblings, husband, and I were not surprised that he desired to contend for his life until his last breath. He was one of the many gritty WWII veterans—a fighter—so such a choice did not shock us. Through this difficult season, as a family, we drew closer together, which was a tremendous blessing.

I have learned in my counseling studies that with grief, people recover and make progress at different rates. Typically, people will console those who have lost loved ones for approximately 6-7 weeks. It can take 18-24 months for grief to process but can be longer depending on the individual and the circumstances surrounding the death. It's important to stay in touch with those who are experiencing loss and grief—to allow them the opportunity to talk while earnestly listening. It's not necessary to probe, pry, or prompt these folks. It is sufficient to allow them to open dialogue with those they feel comfortable.

Helpful Suggestions for Those Who Grieve:
* Do not isolate yourself.

- Find a trusted someone in which to candidly share.
- Be straightforward before the Lord, express honest thoughts and feelings as you meet Him in prayer and have a notebook ready to jot heavenly promptings.
- Track your progress using dates, to look back on and be encouraged, as you journal in the healing process.
- Be aware of what the Lord has for you in the days ahead—you have a hope and a future.
- Reach out to a trusted clergy member or counseling professional for broader support if you're stuck at any point in your journey, lingering in a place of depression or regression.

Helpful Suggestions for Those Who Comfort:
- Be there.
- Be faithful.
- Be sensitive and conscientious as you meet with individuals.
- Be filled with the Lord's strength so you can listen and minister.
- Listen to verbal and nonverbal conversation.
- Do not offer advice unless it's requested.
- Discuss the option, with sensitivity to the Holy Spirit, of seeing a professional if a person seems stuck in depression or regression.
- Stay in touch as best you can for months after the loss—possibly years.
- Do not tell people how to feel or that you know how they feel.
- Listen well.
- Speak only when necessary.

God's goodness and benevolence do not come to a screeching halt after we weather grief. I receive regular comfort through God's Word in Jeremiah 29:11 ESV, "For I know the plans I have for you, declares the LORD, plans for welfare and not for evil, to give you a future and a hope."

It's my prayer that in all stages of life we can reach out and receive God's faithful consideration toward us and minister it to others. We can be certain we do not walk this road of life—and loss—alone.

Consider:

What did you gain from this reading that will help with your grief or assist you to minister comfort to another in their time of grief or loss? Journal these ideas. Initiate supportive measures to console others.

Prayer:

Father, thank You for tending lonely hearts and for surrounding us with caring people in our seasons of grief and loss. May our hearts and ears be sensitive and Holy Spirit-focused when we have the privilege of being with one who grieves. Amen.

Cultivating Written Words

Write the vision; make it plain on tablets,
so he may run who reads it.
Habakkuk 2:2 ESV

Have you ever thought about writing to make plain your love for your family or those close to you? The prophet Habakkuk did that with the Word of the Lord to His people as a demonstration of His love for them so they could run well their race in this life. You can do that with your words to those you love.

I still have the letters my beloved parents sent me, and those I returned to them, when I was in the military. I can still see myself peering into my small mailbox on the military base elated to spy incoming letters tucked there. The fact that both parents included a message, even brief ones, meant the world to me. We exchanged written words for more than four years. Stationed in another country, away from all things familiar and lonely at times, a letter in the mailbox made everything hopeful. Our correspondence secured our family bond and clarified the mutual love we shared.

I took this into my own life and ran with it as a parent with my children. For example, soon after my daughter returned from a mission trip, I awakened one morning at

6:00a.m. with a poem in my thoughts. I am not what I'd call a poet, but my heart had been inspired by her experience and words, as from the Holy Spirit, formed in my head. Even though it was a brief trip, she touched less-privileged children's lives in ways that she, and they, will always remember: a relatable smile, a tenderhearted embrace, a meal served with caring hands.

I knew I had to jot down the words in my head right away before they slipped away. I had to write it down and run with it. In the dark, as I hung off the side of my bed with notepad and pencil, I tried not to wake my husband. It took only a few minutes to record my thoughts which I eventually fine tuned into a meditative gift to honor her willingness to serve on a short term mission trip.

In another instance a few years ago, I felt impressed to send my older siblings detailed, personal letters as Christmas gifts. In those letters, I recalled the numerous ways their lives had impacted mine. I shared memories of things they had done for or given me that demonstrated their love and touched me in a special way as a youngster:

- My first Barbie doll that my sister gave me and how delightful it was to dress her up untold times.
- My first tennis racket that my brother gave me which opened up a whole new world for me.
- Times shared sipping cherry cokes while downtown. The cokes were yum, but the intimate experience of visiting the tearoom with my big sis felt very mature.

I wrote of the many selfless expressions they shared with me of who they were and how they loved. I recorded remembrances which revealed their irreproachable character that affected me as I grew. These written letters produced clarity in my mind of those formative years and deepened my appreciation and love for them.

Have you ever thought to draft undeclared sentiments in letters like that for your family members, spouse, children, and/or grandchildren? Using your pen and the written word in such a way signifies your thankfulness and endearment with regard to them. Demonstrations like this of your affection and consideration can be a part of your personal legacy.

Consider:

How can you cultivate written words in periodic letters or cheery notes to your children/grandchildren? Pray about how you can write a song and/or poem about them—cute or reflective—and gift it to them on a special occasion when other family members are present.

Prayer:

Father, help us with meaningful ways to cement lasting impressions upon our loved ones near and far through the power of written expression. Amen.

PRUNING

The necessity to
cut back and trim
that which hinders
spiritual health and fruitfulness
in our lives.

Cultivating Circumspect Living

Look carefully then how you walk, not as unwise but as wise,
making the best use of the time, because the days are evil.
Ephesians 5:15-16 ESV

Not long ago, my husband and I enjoyed a restful vacation in Niagara Falls. We lodged at the Niagara Falls Air Force Base and saw airmen and women training daily, eating in the chow hall, and maneuvering about the base. Most were young, fit, and mission minded.

My mind flashed back to my younger days—my late teens and early twenties when I was on the military base—young, fit, and mission minded at that age. I was one of them. Yesterday.

Well, yesterday was more than forty years ago and it feels like they've just streaked by!

Much has been accomplished in my life through those years—though not without trials and challenges. My post-military training and serving led to forty-plus years of learning how to do happily married life with a faithful husband, decades raising and treasuring our two children, and twenty years touching the lives of classroom children. For many years I appreciated the invigorating challenge of college study, tutoring, and mentoring college students. Peppered in between I engaged in nurse-aid training, hospital volunteerism, and authored articles and books.

All the opportunities in life that God opened for me provided valuable experience for each future life-season and connected me with people. I discovered how to better see and feel life through others' eyes and hearts. These divine assignments allowed my influence to make a difference. Forty years of wisdom-building escorted me to where I am today—still on assignment!

Whatever age you are, whatever stage of life you're in—youth, mature, senior—salute the call and inspiration God has placed upon your heart and life. Take the gift of 168 hours in each week to unmask God's dream for you as you seek His face. Live circumspectly, vigilant with wisdom.

Similar to a child who follows her father's instruction, may we follow the Holy Spirit's leading in every facet of our lives. I appeal to young people—and not-so-young people—to resist squandering time and living. This is not a proposal to just be busy but a call to be about our Father's business—at age 18 or 80.

After our life's journey, according to the affirmation from Matthew 25:21, let's hear God say, "Well done, my good and faithful servant. You have been faithful in handling this small amount, so now I will give you many more responsibilities. Let's celebrate together!"

God's business for us unearths daily adventures. Let's seize them with wisdom, purpose, and passion!

Consider:
What half-started pursuit lies dormant in your innermost core? What mission or project ignites you, nudging your heart? How can you better respect the time God has given you on this earth? Journal your thoughts with anticipation and then proceed with pursuit!

Further Reading:
Life is brief—Psalm 39:4-5; Psalm 103:15-16
Our days are like a passing shadow—Psalm 144:3-4
Our life is like a morning fog—James 4:14

Prayer:
Father, we are reminded in Psalm 103 that our days are like wildflowers—temporary and fleeting. May we wisely live each day walking circumspectly with thankful hearts and appreciation for the gift of time and life. Amen.

Cultivating Godly Life Choices

Today I have given you the choice between life and death, between blessings and curses. Now I call on heaven and earth to witness the choice you make. Oh, that you would choose life, so that you and your descendants might live!
Deuteronomy 30:19 NLT

It's a solemn thought to ponder how the God of the universe grants us the free will to choose our way in this world. How freeing—yet fragile.

The daily choices you and I make matter. A lot. Our choices matter for more than ourselves. The lives of others are impacted daily by our free will. God's Word guides us in His will for our lives and daily we are faced with choices for blessing or cursing (good or ill), that may play out to an eternal choice for life or death—and not just for ourselves.

For instance, my answer to God's call to follow Him many years ago made all the difference in who I married, the way I parented my children, the college/career path I chose, and the selection of friends with whom I formed relationships.

My Spouse:
The Christian man I chose to marry was God-fearing and filled with integrity. There were no surprises behind the honest man he presented himself to be. The stability of our

169

marriage is ultimately due to our relationship in Christ. My marriage to a man who loves both Christ and me is a beautiful combination with daily rewards.

My Children:

As parents, we followed the Scriptures' instruction to train our children in the ways of the Lord, including church attendance and a Christian school experience. Far from perfect in our foibles, we did our best to love and train them according to the guidance of Scripture which proved conducive to their embrace of Jesus as their personal Savior and Lord.

My College Training:

My choice of major and courses studied in school, that were within my power, were not anti-God and did not confuse or corrupt the Word of God I cultivated in my life. Safeguarding my biblical worldview continues to transform my heart and mind to God's way of doing life.

My Friends:

I formed close friendships with those who shared a like-mindset in a desire to grow in relationship with Christ. We sharpened each other in the ways of God and developed committed lifelong platonic relationships.

Because God is very clear that our choices will result in either a blessed life or a cursed one, we must conscientiously choose in all things. The choice I made to marry my spouse affected not only me, but also my immediate family and extended family. Together, he and I have been able to share truths of Scripture with family members.

The children my husband and I had have grown to impact multitudes in their spheres of influence including my husband's and my extended families. Their godly life choices helped individuals with practical needs and spiritually touched souls for Christ.

In addition, as our friends desired to follow God's way of living life, their impact on our children reinforced biblical truth as we interacted with one another.

Though my life has played out with trials and imperfections, my foundational choices to make God central in all things secured an impact of blessing beyond my own life. How we affect the lives of others comes down to our free will in choosing well.

Consider:

What choices do you face today that will impact your future in profound ways? With contemplation, journal these choices and consequences.

Prayer:

Lord, thank You for entrusting us with the freedom of life choices. May we understand the options we make today have the power to also affect our descendants. Amen.

Cultivating Our Goals

Do you not know that in a race all the runners run, but only one receives the prize? So run that you may obtain it.
1 Corinthians 9:24 ESV

Ready, set, goal!

Consider carefully what the Lord would have for us in every season of life. What does He desire for us to become and to accomplish? What must we do to obtain His will for us? Here are four things to remember when we cultivate goals in our lives:

Know That God Loves You

God's love runs deeper than we can imagine—fathomless like Niagara Falls. The gift of Jesus Christ, in both His birth and death, illustrates God's miraculous and merciful love. Although there are numerous passages expressing this love, here are a few of my favorites:

"See what kind of love the Father has given to us, that we should be called children of God; and so we are. The reason why the world does not know us is that it did not know him." 1 John 3:1 ESV

". . . and to know the love of Christ that surpasses knowledge, that you may be filled with all the fullness of God." Ephesians 3:19 ESV

"We love him because he first loved us." 1 John 4:19 ESV

Seek the Lord to Hear His Plan for You

Establish God's objectives for your life and beware of doubts that may assail you like, *I'm too old . . .it's too late . . . I can't do this,* or any other nagging thoughts that attempt to derail you. Resist and proceed. Do not put God in a box regarding new goals for you. Review Psalm 139 from the *New Living Translation Bible* and be heartened as you follow through in His will.

Develop Healthy Habits

Habits begin now. Small things are big things. Often times, minor tweaks are key to significant change. Habit patterns are formed by where we go, with whom we go, and what we do. God is gracious to forewarn us about the danger of associations with those prone to mischief-making and more menacing forms of misconduct.

It is pivotal for us to heed the admonition stated in 1 Corinthians 15:33 ESV, "Do not be deceived: 'Bad company ruins good morals.'" Accepting the offer of a first cigarette may seem innocent and even grown-up, yet it could lead to illicit drug use, alcohol misuse, and ultimately thievery to pay for malignant habits. These simple yet perilous choices can dictate the trajectory of a lifetime.

Choose friends and influencers who hold similar values and cultivate healthy habits such as an interest in going to church and growing in Christ, participating in reaching out to and assisting individuals in need of help, or engaging in wholesome, fun activities such as sports, beach time, mountain exploration, or camping. Habits involving outdoor, fresh air pursuits, physical exercise, temperate appetites, movies or shows loaded with laundered laughter, and living peacefully with others are hardy for one's spirit, soul, and body. The Holy Spirit is present to lead us as we govern our life-time choices.

See Things Through to the Finish

A fortifying quote by the medieval playwright Moliere states, "Men are alike in their promises. It is only in their deeds that they differ." Be strong and courageous, emboldened in deeds to take even a small step forward and begin that thing, make that change, or accomplish unfinished business. Reach that goal and obtain the prize.

Because small things can be big things, the options we choose are significant as we each run our personal races. Follow the still, small voice of the Holy Spirit in your choices. Guard your heart against stubbornness and rebellion. When God's Spirit dwells within us, there's nothing mystical about His lead. He prompts, and we respond.

Embrace the truth of God's love and intentionally seek His aspirations as you cultivate healthy habits and conclude your race with the goal of winning. All these things are purposed for our good and God's glory. Let's run to win!

Consider:

Are you running your race to merely finish or to win? If you want to win, share ways and habits that are necessary to develop and to execute that will yield this victorious result.

Further Reading:

Temperate appetites—1 Corinthians 9:24-26
Laundered laughter—Colossians 3:8
Living peacefully with others—Romans 12:18
Still, small voice of the Holy Spirit—1 Kings 19:11-12

Prayer:

Father, may my days be filled with meaningful passion as I run my distinctive race to reach appointed goals to honor You. Amen.

Cultivating a Loving Heart

By this all people will know that you are my disciples,
if you have love for one another.
John 13:35 ESV

We have a fruit and vegetable garden with berries and the beginnings of some vegetables. My husband planted specific fruits and veggies we hoped to harvest. It's exciting to witness the plants as they emerge from their seed-stage!

Unfortunately, there are more weeds than anything else out there today. This happened because the garden was neglected.

In the same way, it's easy to allow spiritual weeds to sprout up in our hearts if we forsake the plants. Some of these weeds—the works of the flesh listed in Galatians–are jealousy, anger, strife, sorcery, sexual impurity, selfish aspirations, and idolatry. Although some of them are less obvious carnal desires, they are still sinful trespassers. They choke out the fruit and blossoms—the very things our garden was intended to produce. For the plant to thrive, encroaching weeds must be plucked regularly as they try to invade and strangle the good plants.

Ephesians 4 instructs believers to tend the garden of our minds towards righteousness and holiness. We need not be surprised if, and when, we notice corrupting attitudes trying to take root in our heart-gardens. Rather, we must uproot these poisonous intruders as soon as they surface. Once we recognize their presence, decide to abandon the spoiled thoughts and substitute with wholesome mindsets.

Our hearts are like these gardens where God calls us to grow in rightness, good deeds, and love. We must regularly visit our hearts to foster and till them. People identify Christians by their love—acknowledging they are Christ's followers.

As Christians, our dispositions begin in the heart. Our character is conceived in our personal gardens. We first sow the seeds—the inner, private thoughts and ideas. Before we speak something outward, we think about it inward. In Luke 6, Jesus explained what comes out of a person's mouth began as an underlying belief or attitude.

Christ's love fertilizes in the soil of a Christian's heart. It was planted there when we first welcomed Christ into our lives. This agape, unconditional love emanates from God and is associated with God Himself. His love enables us to esteem and love others—believers and unbelievers. God's character is then produced in us in prominent aspects of life: patience, kindness, selflessness, and hopefulness.

- Love *patiently* waits in the grocery or gasoline line, until after the wedding vows are pronounced, and to actively listen first before responding.
- Love is *kind* when she opens her mouth to speak— corrects a child or considers another's opinion.
- Love is *selflessness* when serving at home, work, or church, not controlling every minute detail, or when overlooked for an "atta' girl" affirming word.
- Love is ever *hopeful* when it endures through trials, doesn't quit but hangs on forever, and trusts in God's promises.

If we willingly and actively pursue a love response, we will not grieve the Spirit of God. As Christians, we can react this way because God has placed His agape love in our heart garden.

All people yearn for love. Both unbelievers and believers will recognize us by our love. Jesus taught that God is kind even to the unthankful and wicked. May we allow God to change us into His image, love through us, and touch others with His reflection. It's the way of Love.

Consider:

What thoughts and ideas have you planted in your heart garden? How can you be a reflection of God and His generous love? Think of three people you may have found difficult to love in your past, and actively reach out with God's power and strength.

Further Reading:

The works of the flesh—Galatians 5
The love of God planted in our hearts—Romans 5:5b
Grieve the Spirit of God—Ephesians 4:30a
Create in me a clean heart—Psalm 51:10

Prayer:

Father, thank You for making it possible for us to love others well because of who You are in us. Your love is embedded in our core. We look to represent You accurately as we diligently tend our heart gardens. Amen.

Cultivating a Thankful Heart vs Misplaced Expectations—Part 1

*From his abundance we have all received
one gracious blessing after another.*
John 1:16 NLT

"You're not meeting my needs, and therefore you're not measuring up to my standards and expectations!"

Ouch! Have you ever voiced these words or thoughts in this accusatory manner about your spouse?

I'm guilty and have sorely repented of placing expectations upon my husband that should be reserved for God. The Lord is my all in all—not my husband. To misplace expectations like this on a spouse can result in them feeling like a caged animal, belittled, devalued, and controlled. In contrast, we do well to appreciate our loved one, and thank God for him. He belongs to God, too.

Tell your spouse how much you appreciate his thoughtfulness . . . especially when he brings you flowers—just because. Or when he texts an endearing message to show you he's thinking of you—just because. Or when he slips a little love note in your lunch box, handbag, or suitcase—just because. No ulterior motive.

Acknowledge him, with thankful words, each time he compliments you. Be sure to honor him in his selfless acts of kindness and praise his handyman skills as he partners with you to make your house a home. Just because.

At every opportunity, when we treat our husbands with thankfulness, they soar free, like a bird released from the constraints of a cage and spread their wings with greater ability to love us.

Pastor Keith Moore of Moore Life Ministries said, "Expect nothing and appreciate everything."

People often disappoint us, unable to deliver our desired expectations. But God will always be present for us, able to do above and beyond what we can think or imagine as promised in Ephesians 3:20. His steadfast affection and faithfulness toward us never changes.

Cultivate a thankful heart towards your spouse, children, friends, co-workers, or boss and guard against placing expectations on them that should only be reserved for God. Gratefully expect all things from God, alone. Look to Him, lean on Him, trust in Him, and behold His mighty Hand to meet all your deepest needs.

Doing so frees others to simply love you—and frees you from disappointments, so you can love them unconditionally.

Consider:

If you recognize yourself leaning too hard on people to meet needs and expectations that only God can fulfill, what kind of personal changes can you make? If you've already begun to do this, what improvements have you witnessed?

If you have a spouse who doesn't often offer the thoughtfulness expressed in this message, begin to recognize even the smallest kindness and acknowledge your thankfulness. As you cultivate a grateful heart, both of you will be better off. Always remember God knows it all and looks on the hearts. Our grace-filled actions are never in vain.

Further Reading:
Sacrifices of thanksgiving—Psalm 107:22 NLT

Prayer:
Father, thank You for giving me my spouse and many other special people in my life. Help me look to You, though, to receive what only You can provide in my life. I confidently rest in You because I know You always attend to me and are faithful to Your promises. With thanksgiving, amen.

Cultivating a Thankful Heart vs Misplaced Expectations—Part 2

Blessed be the Lord, who daily bears us up; God is our salvation.
Selah
Psalm 68:19 ESV

In Part 1 of this topic, we explored where our expectations should be in cultivating a thankful heart on God and God alone. But what kind of things can we expect from the Lord? How does He meet us in our daily lives, at our deepest need, that we should cultivate a thankful heart towards Him?

Here are some things we can confidently expect from God, with thanksgiving. Meditate upon and declare them aloud:

- With a thankful heart, I can expect from God His kindness towards me because His Word says in Psalm 117:2 NLT, *"For his unfailing love for us is powerful; the Lord's faithfulness endures forever. Praise the Lord!"*
- With a thankful heart, I can expect God to see me through the valleys of life where the shadow of death lurks, as the Word in Psalm 23:4 NLT declares, *"Even when I walk through the darkest valley, I will not be afraid, for you are close beside me. Your rod and your staff protect and comfort me."*

- With a thankful heart, I can expect God will work out all my trials in life for good as He tells me in James 1:3-4 NLT, *". . . whenever trouble comes my way, let it be an opportunity for joy. For when my faith is tested, my endurance has a chance to grow."*

- With a thankful heart, I can expect God to fulfill all His promises as the Bible states in 2 Corinthians 1:20 ESV, *"For all the promises of God find their Yes in him. That is why it is through him that we utter our Amen to God for his glory."*

- With a thankful heart, I can expect complete assurance from the Lord that on the cross, Jesus took my infirmities and pains. He did this so I can rest in Him when I pray for comfort and healing, proclaiming in Isaiah 53:4-5 NLT, *"Yet it was our weaknesses He carried; it was our sorrows that weighed Him down. And we thought His troubles were a punishment from God, a punishment for His own sins! But He was pierced for our rebellion, crushed for our sins. He was beaten so we could be whole. He was whipped so we could be healed."*

- With a thankful heart, I can expect that God hears me in prayer and responds to me because 1 John 5:14-15 NLT states, *"And we can be confident that He will listen to us whenever we ask Him for anything in line with His will. And if we know He is listening when we make our requests, we can be sure that He will give us what we ask for."*

- With a thankful heart, I can expect that I'll never be
  left alone because the Bible tells me in Hebrews 13:5b
  NLT, *"I will never fail you. I will never abandon you."*

These few examples illustrate the guarantee that our
heavenly Father is faithful to honor His Scriptural promises.
With grateful hearts we can securely put our expectations
and hope in Him.

Consider:
What promises of God have you seen manifested in your
life? How did God's fulfillment of your needs and
expectations energize you and build your faith? As you read
your Bible, search for other Scriptures you can deposit in
your heart so you cultivate trusting and grateful
expectations.

Prayer:
*Father, I'm grateful for the many benefits You continually lavish
upon me as You bear me up even in the dark valleys. I can
thankfully look to You in expectation that You always attend to
me and are faithful to Your promises. Amen.*

Cultivating Our Victorious Default

Those who live in the shelter of the Most High
will find rest in the shadow of the Almighty.
This I declare about the Lord:
He alone is my refuge, my place of safety;
he is my God, and I trust him.
Psalm 91:1-2 NLT

What's our default when we're confronted with challenging circumstances? Is it fear or is it faith?

I was challenged with this question and experience when my husband and I walked past the house with two ferocious dogs—big, brawny, bold, and brash. With our little Cairn Terrier in tow, these two bully dogs with their menacing barks would jump on their dilapidated, wooden fence as we passed their house. It unnerved me when the rickety fence wobbled as the dogs pounced up against it, charging from one end of the yard to the other.

As we rounded that corner of our daily trek, I often felt uneasy. Fear tried to grip me. I'd silently pray and strategize my plan of action as to how I would react if the scary dogs got loose. *I'll scoop up my 13-pound Keira into my left arm and use the Name of Jesus as my weapon—the Name above every other name.*

Our usually pleasant walk began to feel rather unpleasant as I anticipated that particular section of the two-mile walk. It occurred to me that my default had become fear-driven and fear-based. On one or two occasions, if my husband weren't able to walk with us, I took a different route. If I did walk that way, I hoped the dogs would be inside.

In time, the Lord spoke to my heart, *Is your default fear or faith?* His Spirit rose up within me and a rush of faith climbed up in my heart. I took authority of that invasive fear and faith exchanged places! Free and victorious, I enjoyed our daily walks once again.

With new boldness as I approach that property, I whisper, *Lord, I trust You and thank You for protecting me as I pass this house. Thank You for Your angels who are here to minister on my behalf.* I still use the Name of Jesus as I near the property, too, but the spirit of fear is no longer king. My new victorious default is faith—not fear.

To cultivate our prevailing default of faith, instead of nursing defeatist thoughts, we can think and speak aloud:

- Romans 8:31—*If you are for us and with us, God, then who can be against us?*
- 1 Corinthians 15:57—*God gives us victory in life through Jesus Christ.*
- Psalm 34:4—*As we seek You, Lord, You respond to us and deliver us from unconfirmed fears.*
- Psalm 91:11—*You give Your angels charge over us, Lord, to keep us in all situations.*

Whether it's bully dogs or other intruding thieves, with Jesus' Name, the angels, and God's presence, we can triumphantly default to faith!

Consider:

When fear barks at you, what faith steps can you grasp to quench the bite? If hounding fears torment you, call on the Lord for rescue and deliverance. Take decisive action with His help to overcome in order to live victoriously.

Further Reading:

God's protection for His people—Psalm 91
God's nearness, goodness, & faithfulness—Psalm 34
Victory is ours through Christ—Romans 8:37

Prayer:

Father, may I default to faith versus fear when bully dogs try to hold me captive. As I choose to make You my fortress and refuge, I'm assured You will keep me safe. My security and rest are found in You. Thank You forever. Amen.

Cultivating Self-Control

But the Holy Spirit produces this kind of fruit in our lives: love,
joy, peace, patience, kindness, goodness, faithfulness,
gentleness, and self-control.
Galatians 5:22-23a NLT

I did it God's way . . .

Living a life within self-controlled boundaries may sound like a caged existence, but it's just the opposite. It's a life of freedom.

Growing up, there was a boy in my school who resisted the teacher's class rules. He persisted to stubbornly misbehave. This classmate refused to control himself and caused disruption for the teacher and the rest of the class. The teacher constantly heeded to stop teaching, speak to him, and occasionally usher him to the hallway. His impetuous conduct and decisions swiveled a peaceful classroom atmosphere into chaos and havoc. Perhaps he thought his rebellion against his teacher would lead to freedom, but instead his privileges were revoked and his friendships few.

The wisdom found in Proverbs 25:28 explains that when we don't control ourselves, we are like a city without defense with broken-down walls. We are alerted to our vulnerability, open to attack from the enemy.

The word for self-control in the *King James Bible* is temperance. In the Greek, temperance refers to abstinence in all areas of our lives. This includes our habitual behaviors including what and when we eat and drink, materials we read, friends and relationships we choose, and financial decisions we practice.

The decisions and habits we adopt for ourselves are similar to an athlete's motivation to win a race by setting a goal to commit to conscientious training. If we focus on our goal to achieve God's highest intention for our lives, it fortifies and enables us to proceed with self-control.

Self-control encourages us to:

- Forsake self-lordship by yielding ourselves to God–hold His hand.
- Focus on our goal to accomplish God's purpose–grasp His dream for us.
- Discipline to train ourselves according to our goals–drill masterly.
- Run to win our life's race–finish well.

Self-control is a fruit of the Holy Spirit, cultivated when we decide to be led by Him, restrain our flesh, and choose to walk in obedience to God's direction—His promptings. As we follow His lead, we won't comply with the cravings of the flesh. It may feel like a tug-of-war competition, but once we yield to the Holy Spirit, He empowers us to deny our natural man's pull to dominate. He enables us to control our desires, appetites, and ultimately our decisions.

With God Almighty, the great I AM in your heart, you can shut the door on the enemy's lies that whisper you cannot control yourself. Don't allow this day to pass until you've humbly met with God to express your surrender of the challenges that handcuff you. In this way, mastering self-control is within our reach.

Consider:
Explain how the Holy Spirit empowers you to overcome troublesome areas in your life. If you're challenged with controlling yourself in specific ways, surrender your attitude and the obstacles to God. He will meet you at your point of need.

Further Reading:
Run to win the prize—1 Corinthians 9:24-27
God working in us—Philippians 2:12-13

Prayer:
Father, thank You for producing the fruit of self-control in our lives as we submit ourselves to You. When we do this, we live a life of advantage and liberty. Amen.

Cultivating Healthy Self-Love

You shall love your neighbor as yourself.
Matthew 22:39b ESV

Before I love me, it's best to love Thee.

God's love goes before us in all things and blankets the details of our lives.

When I was discharged from the military, having served almost four years in Europe and ultimately in Italy, God revealed Himself to me in a powerful way. Using the yellow pages of a telephone book, He led me to a church three blocks from home. It became a spiritual support and stabilizing force in my life for the next year. He gave me new friends from that assembly that filled the void as I had lost touch with hometown friends, the community, and everything civilian. In a sense, I needed to start over — employment, transportation, relationships, and church.

Fresh home from my time in Italy, I was amazed to see that many of the church's congregants were mature Italian believers who earnestly loved God! We immediately embraced each other and developed warmhearted friendships. With a grateful heart I continued to learn about God's love for me. I was a new Christian reunited with my loving parents and family, but I also connected with a gracious church fellowship.

Zephaniah 3:17 proclaims that God rejoices over me and stills my soul with His compassionate love. He disciplines me without condemnation, and even used a telephone directory to tether me to complete strangers—a new church family—who welcomed me with no strings attached.

God's Love for Me—Foundational

Before I can love myself or others it's important to know how much God loves me. His love is cavernous and free—we don't and can't earn it. His love heals and completes us. His love is relational: God knows what we think and who we are in the private recesses of our heart. The depth and breadth of His love for us is beyond measure as illustrated in Matthew 10:30 where even the hairs of our head are numbered.

God's supply of love is greater than our demand. It is unconditional, unwavering, and boundless, like a boulder that you can't budge, re-locate, or change its steel-like presence. God loved all of humanity when Jesus went to the cross to die, but even if it had been for just one person, He would have offered Himself for that one.

My Self-Love—Progressive

Self-love is cultivated in stages. The thoughts we believe about ourselves and the ruminations that occupy our mind and time are king-like and often guide our behavior.

When we're growing up, we may internalize erroneous statements or perceptions such as: *You'll never accomplish that goal* or *You're less than—not enough.* We conceivably drag these destructive thoughts into our adult lives like a snow-laden sled up a steep slope. They encumber our climb through life if we don't dump them so we can advance to the peaks of the healthy love for self God called us to.

To battle these lies, we must replace them with God's truth according to His Word, the Bible: *You were made in My image; You're more than a conqueror; I delight in you, my precious child.* Remaining patient, we meditate on God's loving affirmations embracing them as our own. He treasures us. When I understand God loves me, I'm liberated to love myself. First John 4:19 affirms that we possess the ability to love because God first loved us.

Self-love is not selfish as I once thought. It fuels me with a spiritual and physical diet that strengthens, sustains, and satisfies my whole being. This leads to a desire to support brothers and sisters in the faith and everyone else in my life. When God meets my need for His love, I am free to liberally love others. I stop thinking about what I need or what I desire and place my focus outward rather than inward. God's love and care of me frees me to demonstrate His love and affection for others—loving my neighbor as myself. This may resemble:

- Remembering someone in prayer
- Providing a listening ear
- Delivering a meal
- Sharing a visit with a lonely soul
- Offering an afternoon of counsel
- Writing and sending a merry note
- Being present as whatever need in another's life arises

I recall a social media meme that read, *Remember to take care of yourself, you cannot pour from an empty cup.*

I've made it a point to earmark time to exercise my body and strengthen it for the purposes God ordains. I rest my body, mind, and soul and allow margin in my schedule for balance. As we are reminded each time we board an airplane, we must put our oxygen mask on first before we try to position one on our child. We are helpless to help others without first caring for ourselves. Fill up to prepare to be emptied out.

Enjoy My Life—Prevailing Contentment

I prefer to see life as half-full. I may not always feel that way, but I choose half-full over half empty. It's a blessed life crowded with satisfaction.

Loving myself includes doing what I enjoy with leisure. Sometimes it's alone and other times with those whom I cherish, those who fill my love tank. These people nourish my emotional and relational self.

Some favorite self-love activities:

- Neighborhood walks
- Boardwalk strolls or power walks
- Summer concerts and speakers at the seashore
- Reminiscent excursions to military bases with my husband
- Vacays in unfamiliar surroundings to invigorate the soul, mind, and body
- Staycays at home adoring a good read or hanging around the house with no specific agenda
- Occasional movies, preferably real-life stories packed with messages of possibility, hope, and heroic take-aways
- Consignment shops with unrestricted time limits to uncover treasures

- Occasional restaurant dates
- Meaningful conversations–iron sharpens iron
- Sharing God's love–exposing the truth of His character, existence, and access
- Visits to Hallmark Shops—notecard paradise—my supply may last 'til eternity

When I practice healthy self-love with margin in my schedule, I feel fulfilled and refreshed. It is an abundant life!

Consider:
What are some measures you implement or apply to cultivate healthy self-love? Describe how you balance love for yourself with love for God and love for your neighbor. Further explore these ideas with a small group for robust and sharpened discussion and encouragement.

Further Reading:
We're made in God's image—Genesis 1:27
We're more than conquerors—Romans 8:37
We're God's delight—Psalm 18:19
The Great Commandments—Matthew 22:34-40
God's always known us—Psalm 139:13-16
Seek God's Kingdom first—Matthew 6:33
Iron sharpens iron—Proverbs 27:17

Prayer:
Father, help me to continue to know Your love for me in more intimate ways, so I can better love others. I recognize the daily benefits and mercies You impart. I live a blessed life, secured in healthy self-love, and am thankful that Your loving goodness is unparalleled. Amen.

Cultivating Promise-Centered Self-Talk

For nothing will be impossible with God.
Luke 1:37 ESV

When I was in college years ago, I wrestled with trigonometry. I needed to master this class for my degree. I exercised healthy self-talk before it was commonplace practice with a resolve not to quit. *God will see me through this difficult place. I will conquer this challenge.*

After asking the professor for help, he directed me to a tutor. The tutor and I were not compatible. Telling me the answers didn't help the how-we-get-there process. I felt like I was losing the limited footing I had, and the semester-clock was ticking at full speed ahead. I had to resist nagging negative thoughts knocking at the entrance to my mind such as, *How do you expect to conquer this when you didn't take the preparatory courses years ago?*

While I persisted with assignments, still without full comprehension, I desperately prayed and continued to persevere until—Hallelujah! God opened my mind to the understanding I needed. He showed me how to study, when to study, and where to study. I practically aced the final comprehensive exam completing the course with an A+ average. It was a significant personal testimony of His help in my time of trouble. God gets all the glory.

We cultivate sanctified, promise-centered self-talk as we integrate godly self-talk to pursue bigger-than-possible undertakings. If we don't, negative self-talk plants within our hearts seeds of doubt and can't. Thoughts and seeds that materialize to steal possibility and joy.

When we exercise healthy self-talk in line with God's Word and promises, Philippians 4:13 ESV reassures that, *"[We] can do all things through [Christ] who strengthens [us]."* Some Promise-Centered Self-Talk Starters to cultivate a renewed mind in Christ Jesus:

- *. . . for I have learned how to get along happily whether I have much or little.* (Philippians 4:11b NLT) This may need to be learned and then practiced, but we can live contentedly regardless of circumstances.

- *The Lord protects me from danger—so why should I tremble?* (Psalm 27:1b NLT) In Christ, I am secure.

- *Give all your worries and cares to God, for he cares about what happens to you.* (1 Peter 5:7 NLT) We're not built for the worries; He is.

- *Don't worry about anything; instead, pray about everything. Tell God what you need and thank him for all he has done. If you do this, you will experience God's peace . . .* (Philippians 4:6-7a NLT) Live with a thankful heart.

- *And hope does not put us to shame, because God's love has been poured into our hearts through the Holy Spirit who has been given to us.* (Romans 5:5 ESV) Therefore, I have the ability through Christ to love others.

- *For the word of God is full of living power. It is sharper than the sharpest knife, cutting deep into our innermost thoughts and desires. It exposes us for what we really are.* (Hebrews 4:12 NLT) Scripture is alive and effectual.

- *Always be joyful.* (1 Thessalonians 5:16 NLT) This is a strong exhortation, often done sacrificially, yet when we rely on Jesus, He bolsters us.
- *And my God will supply every need of yours according to His riches in glory in Christ Jesus.* (Philippians 4:19 ESV) Pray and ask God for wisdom to creatively generate income using your skills. Do the one thing — the next thing — you think you should, to create forward action.
- *He forgives all my sins . . .* (Psalm 103:3a NLT) Once we ask for forgiveness, He forgives us and we're pardoned.
- *[He] heals all [our] diseases . . .* (Psalm 103:3b NLT) Sometimes immediately, while sometimes we prevail in due season. Trust, pray, and obey.

When the task or commission before you is God-ordained, it's achievable. My specific challenge — a math class — may have sounded like a simple situation to you. But what are the hurdles that linger in the recesses of your mind that come to de-stabilize your footing? *The prospect of starting a home-based business? Enlistment in military service? The undertaking of child adoption? The prompt to proceed with a missionary calling?*

As you cultivate your healthy self-talk, always remember nothing will be impossible with God.

Consider:
What Promise-Centered Self Talk Starters will you meditate on to strengthen your faith and build your spirit? Begin with finding and meditating on one Scriptural promise of God. Think about it and cultivate your self-talk around the promised possibility. Our lives can be more blessed if we

believe God for His promises and live on the 'can believe/can receive' side of life.

Further Reading:
Help in time of trouble—Psalm 46
God's benefits—Psalm 103
Abide in Christ—John 15
Transformed by the renewal of our minds—Romans 12:2
Casting down imaginations—2 Corinthians 10:5a

Prayer: *Father, as I depend on You for Your strength and ability, may I discover possibilities I never dreamed of before. Thank You. Amen.*

Helpful References

Through the years, I've received wisdom and teaching from many sources. The references below informed some of the content in this book.

Rollins, Jess. November 16, 2016, *Leash Training: How to Walk a Dog that Pulls*. Pet Expertise. https://bit.ly/3D1alE9

Zak, George. March 30, 2021, *Courting a Catastrophe. The Daily Journal*. Vineland, NJ newspaper.

Bosworth, F. F. (2006) *Christ the Healer*. Grand Rapids, MI: Baker Publishing Group, 9th Edition.

Tobias, Cynthia. (1998) *The Way They Learn*. Focus on the Family Publishing.

Tobias, Cynthia. *Discovering Your Child's Learning Style (Part 1 of 2)*, www.focusonthefamily.com. Original air date 8-8-2013.

Clinton, Tim & Langberg, Diane. (2011) *The Quick-Reference Guide to Counseling Women*. Grand Rapids, MI: Baker Books.

Dobson, James. (1998). *Complete Marriage and Family: Home Reference Guide*. Eugene, OR: Harvest House Publishers.

Petersen, Jim. (2007) *Why Don't We Listen Better? Communicating & Connecting in Relationships*. Portland, OR: Petersen Publications.

Tales with Morals, www.taleswithmorals.com *Aesop Fables: The Ant and the Grasshopper*, https://bit.ly/3Iyu0fN

Wright, H. Norman. (2011) *The Complete Guide to Crisis & Trauma Counseling.* Bloomington, MN: Bethany House Publishers.

Diorio, MaryAnn. (2021) *The Iron Saint.* Merchantville, NJ: MaryAnn Diorio Books.

Hagin, Kenneth E. (1997) *What to Do When Faith Seems Weak and Victory Lost.* Tulsa, OK: Kenneth Hagin Ministries, Inc.

Groeschel, Craig. (2010) *The Christian Atheist.* Grand Rapids, MI: Zondervan.

DeMoss Wolgemuth, Nancy. (2018) *Lies Women Believe: And the Truth that Sets Them Free.* Chicago, IL: Moody Publishers.

Chan, Francis & Lisa. (2014) *You and Me Forever: Marriage in Light of Eternity.* San Francisco, CA: Claire Love Publishing.

Colbert, Don. (2008) *Stress Less.* Lake Mary, FL: Siloam—A Strang Company.

Spurgeon, Charles. (n.d.). *Morning and Evening.*

GLOW—**G**o **L**ove **O**thers **W**ell from Missionary & Author, Dar Draper

About the Author

 Christine Strittmatter is a wife, mom, teacher, military veteran, mentor, and writer who is passionate about sharing Scriptural truths with women and children via personal meetings and writings. Chris enjoyed teaching for 20 years at a Christian school and currently serves in a support-staff role at Fairton Christian Center and Academy. She has recently received her Master's in Human Services—Marriage and Family studies from Liberty University. In addition, she received master's certifications from LU in Pastoral Counseling and Military Resilience.

Being a mom to her two grown children has been Chris' primary mission in life. She has had articles published in New Jersey Family Magazine three consecutive years, 2013-2015. In her first book, *The Real Life Mom: 96 Inspirational Insights and Stories for Mothers*, she shared real life snippets to inspire, encourage, and challenge others in their everyday walks with God. *The Real Life Mom: 52 Devotions to Cultivate Fruitful Living* is her latest work culled from years of devotional writings and journals.

Chris and her chivalrous husband, Dave, continue to appreciate sharing a blessed Real Life together for the past 42 years.

Book Shepherding Services

by Kathryn Ross
Pageant Wagon Publishing

Let me help you develop the book
God is calling you to write ~

From Idea to Finished Product!

A la carte and bundle services
include:
~ Monthly Consulting Sessions
~ Editing
~ Layout & Design
~ Print Publishing
~Audio Book Recording
~ Ghostwriting

www.pageantwagonpublishing.com

Made in USA - North Chelmsford, MA
1327413_9781736008027
09.28.2022 1238